Horrockses Fashions

Off-the-Peg Style in the '40s and '50s

Horrockses Fashions

Off-the-Peg Style in the '40s and '50s

Christine Boydell

First published by V&A Publishing, 2010
V&A Publishing
Victoria and Albert Museum
South Kensington
London SW7 2RL

Hardback edition
ISBN 978 1 85177 601 6

10 9 8 7 6 5 4 3 2
2014 2013 2012 2011 2010

Designer: Will Webb
Copy-editor: Linda Schofield
Index: Christine Shuttleworth

New V&A photography by Ken Jackson and Paul Robins, V&A Photographic Studio

Front jacket illustration: Selected Horrockses' fabrics based on silhouette of a Horrockses' dress
Back jacket illustration: (left) The Queen wearing one of Horrockses' dresses in New Zealand in
December 1953, (see p.132); (right) A summer dress, (see p.117)
Frontispiece: A strapless cotton cocktail dress in a fabric designed by Eduardo Paolozzi, (see p.97)

Printed in Hong Kong

V&A Publishing
Victoria and Albert Museum
South Kensington
London SW7 2RL
www.vam.ac.uk

Contents

Introduction

'Horrockses Fashions':

A New Ready-to-Wear Label

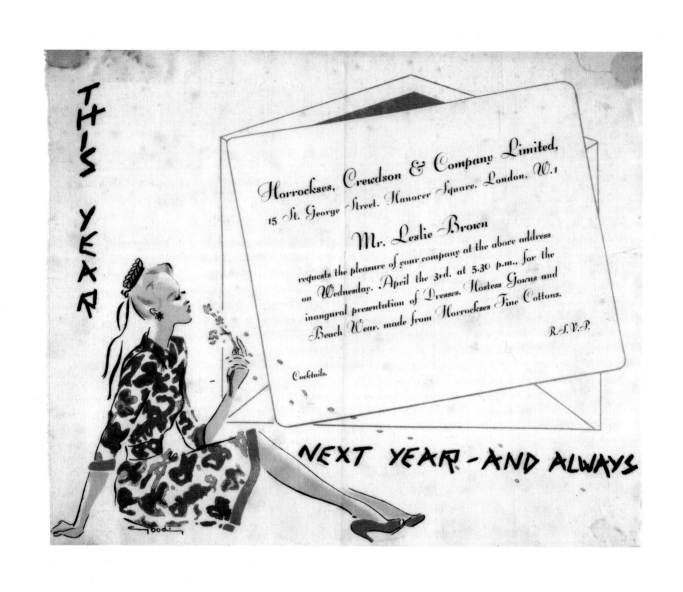

i An invitation to Horrockses' first fashion show in 1946, printed on a lightweight cotton.
Christine Boydell

Horrockses Fashions was established by the well-known Preston-based cotton manufacturer Horrockses, Crewdson & Company Limited as a means of promoting its key product – cotton piece goods. The first collection was launched on 3 April 1946 to enthusiastic reviews (i). *Country Life* described its cotton creations as '...a revolution in fashion; they have the technical perfection as well as the chic that opens up a new market.'[1] The *Evening Standard* fashion correspondent noted that 'Styling apart, the most interesting features were the modern designs and colourings, both equal to those usually associated with printed silks and rayons...',[2] and *The Drapers' Record* commended 'their cotton frocks for their superb cut, good colours and unusual designs.'[3] The collection consisted of cotton beachwear, hostess gowns and dresses (iii), with dresses selling from 2½ to 3 guineas.[4] Early promotion of its products emphasized the role of its fashion stylists, the fabric designs, the quality of the cloth and the fact that it was treated with a process called 'Permanent Crispness', and that colours were fast and the cloth did not shrink (ii). These garments were accompanied by accessories in Horrockses' fabrics: shoes from the Hutton Shoe Company of Northampton and hats by Pissot & Pavey. Careful planning meant that the fashions would be available in the shops at the end of the month and were the realization of the company's intention to 'provide Light-Hearted Clothes made from cotton and other materials, worthy of our tradition'.[5]

The success of Horrockses Fashions was due to a significant marriage of traditional know-how and fashionable innovation. The new label was an unusual example of vertical organization – incorporating cloth production and finished product, via fabric design and fashion styling. This investigation represents the first case study of this kind of company and contributes to the literature on the business history of textiles. The venture was an ambitious plan to extend Horrockses, Crewdson & Co.'s chain of existing production and to associate its established products with new ones, for mutual benefit. The concept for the label demanded careful management of the balance between the practicalities of the ready-to-wear business plan and the creativity of the designers who would provide the up-market fashion upon which the brand would be promoted. The success of this enterprise was dependent on a careful negotiation between the 'exclusive' message inherent in the company's promotion of the brand and the reality of the wide availability of mass-produced fashions.

In order to do this successfully, the Horrockses Fashions' brand needed to be traded on the fabric from which it was made and to carry similar values to the Horrockses' cloth itself – quality and dependability. The company was established at a prescient moment in the history of fashion. Ready-to-wear manufacture had been growing steadily during the period between the two World Wars. The late 1930s saw the establishment of a number of branded women's wear labels, and the Second World War resulted in a more stable and well-organized industry. While Horrockses Fashions became a profitable ready-to-wear concern, with its main output the production of hundreds of units per style, its business strategy involved the creation of a veneer of exclusivity for the brand. It achieved this by following closely Parisian and London

'Horrockses Fashions':

A New Ready-to-Wear Label

Cotton Con

We commend these cotton frocks for their superb unusual designs. The background of this page is a designers' ingenuity. Horrockses, the well-known have made clothes history by producing a cotton crispness and having the fresh finish of linen. here cost from $2\frac{1}{2}$ to $3\frac{1}{2}$ guineas each. Further de

ally suitable for town garden. The map design unusual and so are the eeves, that can be un- ed to nearly elbow length

A graceful gown to wear about the house. The full skirt is topped by a wide sash, and puffed sleeves give a soft shoulder line

good colours and
xample of the fabric
ton manufacturers,
ted for permanent
he models shown
are on page 100

Stripes for summer in
petunia and white, with
well-tailored shoulders,
neat waistline and non-
austerity unpressed pleats

A West African print in
jungle colours, this pina-
fore frock has pants and
brassière to match—ideal
for beach and holiday wear

11

ii *A double-page spread announcing
Horrockses' first collection of cotton
fashions.*
The Drapers' Record, *April 1946*

iii *A publicity photograph from Horrockses Fashions' 1946 collection.*
Christine Boydell

iv *Ruth Addison (centre) wearing a Horrockses' dress on a shopping trip while on holiday in South Africa, early 1950s.*
Ruth Addison

couture styling, by adopting some of its sales and promotional practices, by creating fabric designs exclusive to its brand, by limiting the retail outlets to which it sold, and through carefully considered advertising and promotional campaigns. Such a strategy was to make it one of the most well regarded ready-to-wear labels of the post-war period, both in the industry as a whole and in the minds of the women who wore its products (iv).

This book offers an insight into a particular chapter in the history of Horrockses Fashions. While the brand survived until 1983, the focus of this study is the period 1946 to 1964, its heyday. Setting the company's history in the context of the production and consumption of women's fashions in this

period, it explores not only manufacturing, but also the strategies adopted in selling the fashions, and the responses and reactions of the women who bought them. The intermediaries in the chain between manufacturers and customers are frequently overlooked in histories of the subject, often because there is no surviving evidence documenting their views or actions. Yet, the creation of a brand cannot be understood without them. Fortunately, Horrockses Fashions has left a rich array of source material that brings to life the designers (for the fabrics *and* the garments), fashion photographers, journalists, advertisers and retailers who contributed so much to the company's reputation and success. The study of the company's business

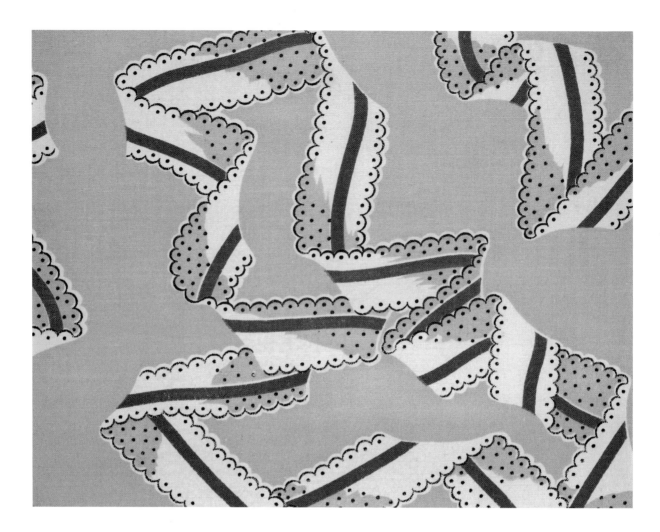

v *A booklet published to accompany*
Horrockses Fashions' second
collection in 1947. It is covered
in an Alastair Morton design.
AAD/1995/16/12/2

records, design archives and interviews with employees and customers (vi) complements what can be learnt from the study of objects in museum and private collections (v), and magazines and trade publications in this reconstruction of the company's story. Each chapter focuses on a phase in the cycle from concept to customer: the first concentrates on the manufacturing environment and the company's structure; the second on the complementary strands of textile and fashion design in the company's strategy; the third on the 'branding' of the end product through various forms of promotion; and the fourth on how retailing met customers' requirements, and how those customers remembered and appreciated their Horrockses' dresses.

vi *A typical Horrockses Fashions'
cotton dress worn by Mrs Elizabeth
Payze as a teenager in
the 1950s, 1953.*
V&A: T.640-1996

15

Introduction

Horrockses Fashions

ther eden

purpose

this seat of

this royal

this royal throne

This

earth of majesty

stone set in a silver

Chapter 1
Exclusivity Off-the-Peg

HORROCKSES, CREWDSON & C° L^TD

SEMPER   EADEM

MANUFACTURE

Horrockses, Crewdson & Company Limited and the launch of a fashion brand

The launch of Horrockses Fashions in 1946 was an attempt by Horrockses, Crewdson & Co. to strengthen its foothold in the business of manufacturing finished goods (1.1). At the time, it already had some experience of garment making with a Manchester-based clothing subsidiary – R.H. Reynolds Brothers Limited, manufacturing overalls and inexpensive women's wear – but this new label was aiming much higher. Horrockses, Crewdson & Co. had a long and distinguished history in the production of fine quality cotton goods. Founded by John Horrocks in 1791, initially it produced cotton yarn and cloth. It soon became the largest manufactory in Preston, Lancashire expanding further throughout the nineteenth century. Its main product was unbleached calico or grey cloth, known as long cloth, which was sold internationally through wholesalers. Horrockses established a reputation for quality cotton cloth and manufacturers who used it would often refer to the Horrockses' name in their advertising. Bloxham and Carr's of Woodbridge Suffolk mention '…Horrockses Long Cloths, Marslands, Shirtings, and 2-yards wide White and Brown Sheeting Calicos, all of which B. and C. beg to observe are of the best quality…'(1.2).[1]

During the nineteenth century, Horrockses began to manufacture dress and household fabrics, its good reputation frequently referred to in the press. In 1887, *The Ladies Treasury* noted that,

1.1 *A Horrockses, Crewdson & Co. label, c.1887.*
Courtesy of the Harris Museum and Art Gallery, Preston.
Photograph by Norwyn Ltd

1.2 *An advertising poster for Horrockses' sheetings, long cloths and flannelettes, 1907.*
The Bowes Museum

1.3 *An advertisement for a range of Horrockses, Crewdson & Co.'s fashion fabrics.*
Film Fashionland, November 1934

1.4 *A 1940s advertisement for Horrockses, Crewdson & Co.'s sheets and towels.*
Image courtesy of The Land of Lost Content

Among goods that never vanish from view are Horrockses' Long Cloth and Sheetings, which have maintained their first-class position for a considerable portion of the century; the reason for this popularity being that they are dependable goods, and have always kept the standard of excellence exhibited at their first introduction.[2]

The company enjoyed a similar reputation for quality abroad, with its first foreign agency established in Portugal in 1823, and another in India in 1830. By the end of the nineteenth century, its products enjoyed a reputation worldwide.

By 1885, Horrockses was selling its own products directly to retailers. These products included sheets, towels, underwear and nightwear. The company considered that the production of finished products was a significant factor in building a reputation for quality, as it allowed more control over how its cotton cloth was used. This is highlighted in comments made by the chairman of the company in 1947,

The reputation for quality and goodwill built up on our branded lines in the past is in small measure due to the freedom of choice of quality and variety offered to us in the purchase of raw cotton, coupled with the advantage of bulk buying at a cost favourable in comparison with world prices. Unlike the majority of spinners and combines in Lancashire who sell their yarns to the grey cloth manufacturer and have little knowledge of their ultimate destination, we are a vertical concern, and as such our cloth carries our name into the homes of those who buy it.[3]

By the twentieth century, Horrockses was using the, less than modest, tag line, 'The Greatest Name in Cotton' in its advertising (1.4).

Before establishing Horrockses Fashions, the parent company's main experience of fashion was the production of dress fabrics for the home dressmaker. These were advertised widely in women's magazines. A 1934 advertisement illustrated the wide range of branded fabrics available, with suggestions for

1.5 *A fashion show at Horrockses,*
Crewdson & Co.'s Manchester
factory, Ivy Mill, in 1946. Betty
Newmarch models a housecoat.
AAD/1995/16/2/2

the customer on the kind of garments best suited to a particular fabric (1.3). For example, 'Horrockses Forella' is described as 'a heavy crepe excellent for dinner and afternoon dresses' which retailed at 2s.11d.[4] Horrockses, Crewdson & Co. owned a number of subsidiaries by the time Horrockses Fashions was launched and it was felt that its healthy trading profit in 1947 was largely down to the progress of these companies. Horrockses Fashions proved to be one of its most successful brands with continual comments in director's reports emphasizing its importance to the company's fortunes.[5]

This was the climate in which Horrockses Fashions was launched (1.5). The key motivating factor of the venture was the promotion of the parent company's cotton cloth and it hoped that by supplying its own subsidiary it would be able to ensure a steady and stable demand for its product. Herbert Mallott, the managing director, explained,

> As the men who made the fabric, we were at the mercy
> of the whims of everyone who handled our output, from
> maker-up to ultimate shopkeeper. And, in my view, our
> fine cottons were not getting the chance they deserved
> because they were not being made into the best
> possible garments.[6]

The decision to produce high-class fashions and to elevate the status of cotton may also have been an attempt to increase sales of its fabric to other clothing manufacturers.

The rise of ready-to-wear

So the launch of Horrockses Fashions, although a large investment for the parent company, was an extension of an expanding portfolio of companies combined with experience in the manufacture and marketing of clothing and fashion fabrics (1.6). The timing of the launch was central to the success

of the venture. Horrockses Fashions had been conceived in 1938 in the context of the growth in the wholesale trade of ready-to-wear women's fashion. Although the Second World War resulted in a long delay before it could put its ideas into action, developments during the intervening years resulted in conditions being even more advantageous for the company.

When Horrockses Fashions was conceived, women had several ways of acquiring their clothes. The wealthy might purchase custom-made outfits from couturiers; many women had clothes specially made by dressmakers or made them themselves; while increasingly women bought from retailers selling ready-to-wear fashions. Women's clothing manufacture had been much slower to transform itself into a fully mechanized factory-based industry than men's wear: fashionability and fit in women's wear had militated against the same rate of mechanization and organized factory production. The purchase of ready-made clothing was usually confined to garments where fit was unimportant, and paying someone to make your clothes suggested a certain status. It was not until the 1920s that the number of small dressmaking and tailoring workshops with craft techniques that had dominated the industry started to decline, and factory production for ready-to-wear gradually took over. Margaret Wray has suggested that there were several factors that encouraged the growth of the wholesale ready-to-wear trade during the 1930s. The simplification of clothing styles during the 1920s was partly responsible, as was the increased availability of inexpensive fabrics such as rayon, which was considered more suitable than the currently available cottons for factory production of reasonably priced clothing. Also significant was the imposition of import duties on cloth and apparel in 1931, which encouraged textile firms to change to the production of lighter cloths more suited for factory production. During the 1930s, the arrival of growing numbers of German and Austrian refugees with appropriate

1.6 *A late 1940s dress, a favourite of its owner, Mavis Bimson. The fabric was designed by Alastair Morton.*
Courtesy of the Harris Museum and Art Gallery, Preston: PRSMG: 1995.140

skills was influential, as was the fact that, following the First World War, changing social structures meant that many better-off women had less time for the fittings required for bespoke clothing.[7]

Improvements to lockstitch, felling, buttonhole and over-locking machines helped to speed up production. The majority of the technical advances in ready-to-wear were established in the USA and found their way to Britain through a number of far-sighted manufacturers. Developments in reliable sizing, planned production and conveyor belt systems were particularly important to the success of ready-to-wear. However, during the 1930s there was still a limited adoption of the sectional and conveyor belt systems of manufacture. The 'individual' or 'making-through' systems dominated, where an individual machinist made a single item. Such a system suited the shorter production runs that governed the manufacture of fashionable women's ready-to-wear.

Initially, ready-to-wear had negative connotations of hastily and shoddily made goods, but gradually standards improved as a number of companies were established manufacturing better quality garments in modern factories, using specific brand identities. For example, Tootal, Broadhurst, Lee Ltd began producing 'Chesro' dresses in its Bolton factory in 1930 in an attempt to sell its cloth, Marldena Ltd opened a new dress factory near Leeds during the decade,

Berketex Ltd began to produce tailored women's wear in 1937, and L. Harris (Harella) Ltd and Windsmoor established factories in London in 1939.[8] Both C&A and Marks & Spencer began to sell ready-made fashions on a large scale in the 1920s. The Wholesale Co-operative Society established its own specialist factories for the production of women's clothing in the 1930s. The trend for companies to establish making-up factories and to produce branded products contributed to Horrockses' decision to do the same.

The ready-to-wear business was classified into three distinct qualities of production: model, medium quality and cheap. Horrockses Fashions straddled the first two (1.7). Model production (sometimes known as wholesale couture) took its influence directly from Paris, but adapted styles to suit mass production techniques. There were few firms operating in this way, but they made a significant impact in terms of fashion and style for the rest of the sector. The company Frederick Starke is an example. Frederick had joined the family fashion business, Madame Starke, in 1927, taking over following his mother's retirement in the 1930s and changing the name of the business to his own (1.8). Another was Rose & Blairman, whose label 'Dorville' was established initially as the name for its imported knitwear. In the late 1920s, it became the brand name for its ready-to-wear range designed by Olive O'Neill. O'Neill is central to the Horrockses' story as she advised the company

1.8 *A Frederick Starke ensemble,*
1952.
V&A: T.643:1 to 5-1996

at the beginning of the Horrockses Fashions venture. She had a wealth of experience in the wholesale trade and during the Second World War she represented that sector of the industry on the committee of the Incorporated Society of London Fashion Designers. She was adept at translating Parisian couture for mass production and introduced American ideas on sizing, grading and manufacture. This experience must have contributed greatly to the early success of Horrockses Fashions and helped to shape its approach to ready-to-wear, with its strong couture connotations. In addition, O'Neill's close working relationship with several textile manufacturers enabled the production of special fabrics for her Dorville fashions.

The growing importance of ready-to-wear was highlighted by the founding of the London Model House Group 1947. The brainchild of Frederick Starke, it was an attempt to unify the efforts of manufacturers in the coordination of the presentation of collections to buyers and suppliers. It was influenced by the Incorporated Society of London Fashion Designers and established to maintain standards for the top end of the fashion industry and to encourage exports of ready-to-wear. These favourable conditions, with a growing acceptance of ready-to-wear, the increasing number of manufacturers producing women's wear and Horrockses, Crewdson & Co.'s previous experience as wholesalers of reasonably priced women's clothing, convinced the company to launch Horrockses Fashions as a means of selling and promoting its cotton cloth. Developments during the Second World War were also to be significant.

The impact of the Second World War
During the Second World War, Horrockses, Crewdson & Co. was involved in the Government's concentration scheme. 'Concentration' involved the voluntary merger of factories in

1.9 *A presentation drawing by Marjorie Field for the haute couture firm Field Rhoades, 1940s.*
V&A: E474.2005

27

order to free up space and production facilities for essential war work. As a result, 60 per cent of Horrockses' factory space was closed down and the production capacity of the company was reduced. During this period, it manufactured cloths required for war purposes as well as Utility fabrics.

It is generally agreed that wartime circumstances contributed to a much better organized clothing industry after the war and a number of Government initiatives were to have a direct impact on the improved production of women's ready-to-wear. Under the broad label of the Utility Scheme, the Government focused on price control, regulation affecting the style of clothing and initiatives to streamline production. Initial regulations were imposed as a means of controlling inflation and to ensure supplies of clothing. Purchase tax on clothing was introduced in October 1940, but removed from Utility clothing in the summer of 1942, resulting in garments that were significantly cheaper than non-Utility. In the following March, the 'Making of Civilian Clothing [Restriction] Orders' or austerity regulations were imposed, which limited the quantity of fabric and trimmings used, requiring manufacturers to re-think designs, and in June 1941 clothing rationing was implemented, restricting the number of items of clothing available for purchase. Couturiers from the recently established Incorporated Society of London Fashion Designers were commissioned to create prototype designs, in order to deflect criticisms that regulations would result in standardized clothing (1.9).[9]

In light of labour shortages and the use of factories for war work, designation schemes were also developed. 'Designation' saw manufacturers cooperate with the Board of Trade and allocate at least 75 per cent of their production to Utility clothing, uniforms or exports – in return they were given ready access to supplies of Utility cloth and labour.[10] Increasing employment, rising wages and the fact that more

1.10 *A 1940s cotton Utility housedress in a floral fabric.*
V&A: T.55-1979

1.11 Ivy Mill, Pin Hill Brow, Ardwick, Manchester, 1958. Photographed by H. Milligan.
Manchester Archives and Local Studies: m11941

women were working with less time to dress-make, improved the demand for ready-made clothing. The Government tended to designate companies that were already reasonably efficient, with making-up organized on sectional and conveyor belt systems, allowing the production of longer runs of a smaller range of styles. Before the war, manufacturers of ready-to-wear averaged 100 garments per style; under the Utility Scheme they were expected to produce at least 1000 (1.10).[11] All clothing made under the Utility Scheme was made using Utility cloth, and because clothing companies needed coupons in order to purchase cloth supplies, only firms who had been able to convert existing stock into coupons were able to manufacture garments. This meant that it was virtually impossible for new companies to launch during this time.

So, ready-to-wear emerged from the war as a much more efficient and prosperous industry, and larger manufacturers had tended to replace less efficient and smaller concerns. Better mass production techniques and more effective costing and sizing practices were encouraged. Austerity regulations resulted in the simplification of styles and the slowing down

of fashionable change, and rationing meant that customers were more demanding in terms of the quality and durability of the limited number of garments they could purchase. Ailsa Garland, a fashion journalist, reported the comments of a man in the coat and suit business on the demands of post-war customers: he complained 'suddenly they want both sleeves the same length'.[12] By the end of the war, 90 per cent of all civilian clothing produced was under the Utility label and a version of the scheme continued until 1952.[13] According to Margaret Wray, women's wear manufacturers enjoyed a prosperous phase between 1946 and 1950, partly due to increased wages resulting in a greater demand for clothing.[14] The involvement of couturiers in the Utility Scheme encouraged many of them to venture into ready-to-wear, including Digby Morton and Peter Russell, and Norman Hartnell began designing for Berketex in 1942. Such associations helped to foreground the role of fashion design in the ready-to-wear industry. But it was the impact of wartime regulation on mass-produced clothing generally that was truly significant.

Horrockses Fashions:
15 St George Street, Hanover Square, London

Horrockses Fashions was well placed in 1946 to launch its brand. With the ending of cloth allocation in 1946, the Utility Scheme lost much of its popularity with manufacturers. Firms who had received regular cloth supplies under designation now had to compete with other manufacturers for supplies. The fact that Horrockses Fashions had a ready supply from the parent company meant it was in a very good position in relation to the competitors. In addition, the doubling of purchase tax on non-Utility clothing in 1947 (to 33⅓ per cent of the wholesale price) increased the demand for Utility cloth and strengthened the position of the cloth supplier, who would often insist on makers-up purchasing a quantity of non-Utility cloth, which they did not really want.[15] Again, in this respect, Horrockses Fashions was favoured by its relationship with Horrockses, Crewdson & Co.

As soon as it was feasible after the war, Horrockses acquired and re-equipped making-up units in Manchester (The Ivy Mill Company) (1.11) and Congleton (W.H. Cliffe & Sons).

Horrockses Fashions
in Fine Cotton

1.12 *An advertisement for Horrockses Fashions.*
Vogue, June 1950

1.13 Betty Newmarch.
AAD/1995/16/1/14

The enterprise was recorded in a director's report:

> We have established at our London Headquarters:
> 15 St George Street, Hanover Square an experienced,
> Designing Staff and fully equipped Show Rooms with
> garments of exclusive design sold through the agency of
> Horrockses Fashions Limited. The response has been
> most gratifying and the organisation will be an
> important factor in bringing quality goods of our own
> manufacture before the public.[16] (1.12)

The staff referred to were a group of individuals with experience in the ready-made fashion trade. The first design director of Horrockses Fashions was Leslie Brown, who had begun his career at British Celanese (a firm specializing in the manufacture of rayon fabric and clothing). The rest of the team came from clothing businesses in Northampton and included two fashion designers, Marta Pirn, an Estonian émigrée, who was the chief designer, and Betty Newmarch, who had begun her career selling clothes wholesale and had modelled during the early years of the company (1.13). Jane Edwardes was in charge of publicity (1.14) and Nell Sharp was experienced in costings and running a sample workroom.

As a fashion-led clothing concern with couture ambitions, it was necessary to have a London base. The parent company already had its sales office in Hanover Square and that location

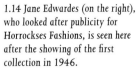

1.14 Jane Edwardes (on the right), who looked after publicity for Horrockses Fashions, is seen here after the showing of the first collection in 1946.
Christine Boydell

1.15 The workroom at 15 St George Street, 1954.
Fabrics and Fashions Overseas, no.2, 1954

1.16 Queen Mary visiting 15 St George Street, Hanover Square in 1948.
AAD/16/4/4

1.17 *Queen Mary visited Horrockses Fashions' London offices in 1948;*
she is seen here feeling the quality of the Horrockses' cotton.
The fabric design is by Alastair Morton.
AAD/1995/16/4/2

proved ideal for Horrockses Fashions, situated as it was between Regent Street and New Bond Street in Mayfair. Horrockses was surrounded by the leading names in fashion. The couturiers Victor Stiebel and Norman Hartnell were close by on Bruton Street, as was the leading ready-to-wear company Frederick Starke and fabric manufacturer West Cumberland Silk Mills (Sekers). Hardy Amies was around the corner on Savile Row, Bianca Mosca on South Audley Street and Peter Russell in Carlos Place.

Number 15 St George Street, a Georgian town house whose stylish interiors were re-designed by Dennis Lennon in time for Horrockses Fashions' launch, provided the kind of couture house connotations of elegance that the firm wanted to emphasize (1.16). The entrance area was dominated by a sweeping staircase that ascended through the centre of the building and flower arrangements were provided weekly by

Constance Spry. It was from this location that Horrockses Fashions' garments were created, samples made, and promotion and sales directed. The ground floor housed Horrockses, Crewdson & Co.'s showroom and the boardroom, while Horrockses Fashions occupied the other floors. The fashion designers were based on the lower ground floor, as was the sample room containing large tables for laying out and cutting patterns (1.15). The salon on the first floor was used to show garments to buyers and with its elegant eighteenth-century proportions, chandeliers and large pier mirrors it provided an atmosphere of grandeur and opulence (1.17). Former employees of the firm speak of the family atmosphere and comment on how hard they all worked, particularly around the seasonal fashion shows, with everyone helping out. Hierarchy was discouraged with everyone from directors to machinists using the main entrance.[17]

1.18 *A typical Horrockses' dress that would have been produced in quantities of up to a 1000, 1959.*
Courtesy of the Harris Museum and Art Gallery, Preston: PRSMG:1996.1000

1.19 *A group of Horrockses Fashions' staff on a day out in the early 1950s. Marta Pirn is third from the left, Betty Newmarch is seated on the right of the front row in the central section.*
Daphne Razzell (née Patten)

From design to finished garment

The manufacture of ready-made fashionable clothing was a complex concern. Predicting what would sell, deciding on volume of production, number of styles and fabric designs per collection, quantities of fabrics required, as well as number and styles of fabric patterns were all crucial. Getting these wrong could result in redundant stock, which, with its high fashion content, would not necessarily be easy to dispose of in the following year. As Horrockses had its own making-up factories, they needed to be kept busy all year, despite the seasonal nature of fashion. Effective production planning was the key to success. Horrockses Fashions had the added complication that it was trying to mass produce merchandize that had connotations of haute couture. The company's marketing emphasized an exclusivity and style that was far removed from the ready-to-wear reality of hundreds of units per style (1.18).

Horrockses Fashions' collections were predominantly made from cotton cloth that had been woven at the parent company's Preston factory, with fabrics designed exclusively for them. These designs were initially provided by the design studio in Preston or purchased from freelance fabric designers and studios. Acquiring designs and organizing printing followed a well-established practice that had operated at Horrockses, Crewdson & Co. for many years (see Chapter 2). To begin with, all the fashions were designed by Marta Pirn and Betty Newmarch (1.19). Pirn had obtained

1.20 *A page from Patricia Hunter's sketchbook 1956–7, showing the cotton fabric design IM3203/4 used for the housecoat (A278).* AAD/16/5/2

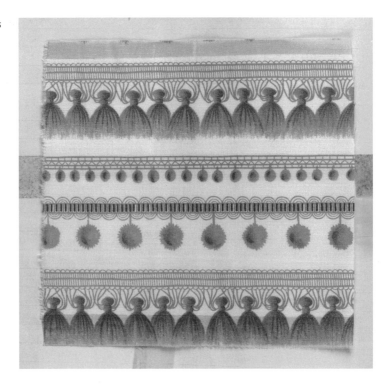

1.21 *A sketch by Patricia Hunter for a housecoat (A278) designed by Betty Newmarch, 1956–7.* AAD/16/5/2

1.22 Horrockses Fashions' graders
and pattern cutters on a trip to
Brighton in the mid-1950s.
Jimmy Peters is on the left.
Jean Grinsted

her design education from lessons in dressmaking and creative handiwork at school in her native Estonia. She was an expert pattern cutter, although sometimes she would use Betty Newmarch's preferred technique of designing on the stand (1.20, 1.21). Newmarch had sold wholesale fashion and had worked in a clothing factory during the war, where she became interested in design. Each fashion designer had their own fitter/cutter and two to three machinists. The designers would choose the fabric patterns they wished to use and their dress designs were passed on to Nell Sharp who ran the sample room with her assistant Pauline Read. They were responsible for producing the master pattern in a size 14 and laying the pattern to achieve the most economical use of the cloth.[18] They also worked out costings for the finished garment, and sourced appropriate trimmings, belts and buttons. Sample machinists made up two finished outfits (one for the showroom and one for the factory – from 1951, a third one was made, for publicity purposes), and fashion design assistant Daphne Patten produced two sketches with samples of the fabric chosen by the designer attached (1.23,

1.24, 1.25). One of the samples along with the pattern, a specification sheet, plus a sketch was then sent to Ivy Mill in Manchester, Horrockses Fashions' principal factory; patterns were graded into different sizes here by Jimmy Peters (1.22). Initially, all Horrockses' styles were made in just three sizes – 12, 14 and 16 – but from 1949 some styles were also produced in size 18; this was fairly typical practice.[19] The sample room, with 10 machinists, was responsible for making prestige items and 'specials', which provided Horrockses Fashions with important opportunities for publicity and helped give the aura of a couture house to the London operations. It was deemed '…of great importance that the Horrockses Fashions' range include some styles of a very high class type which may be difficult to make in a semi-mass production factory and for which the total orders may not be many.'[20] 'Specials' were styles from the main collection that were bought by women who had had an individual introduction to the company, these included a number of actresses, members of the aristocracy and royalty, whom Horrockses felt would help to publicize its creations (see Chapter 3). A 'special' entailed a client choosing

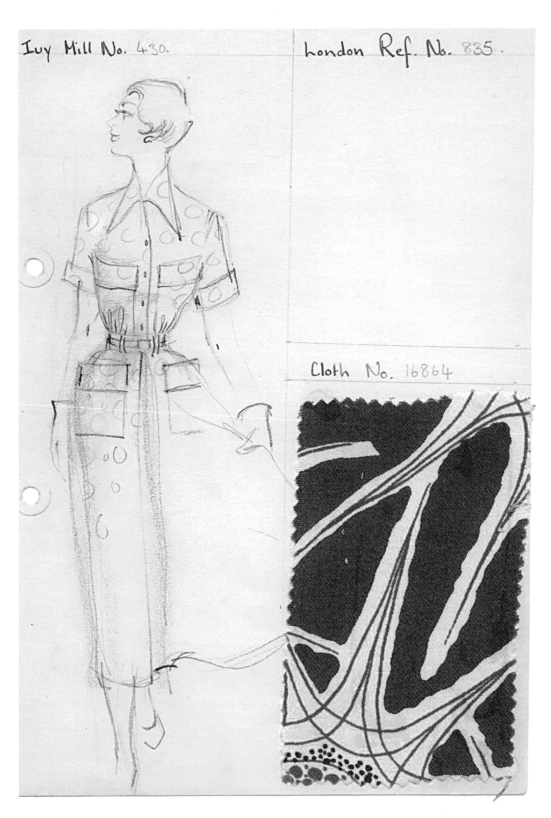

Ivy Mill No. 430.

London Ref. No. 835.

Cloth No. 16864

1.23 *Daphne Patten made two sketches of each finished sample dress. One was retained at George Street and the other was sent to Ivy Mill, along with the sample and pattern. A sample of the fabric chosen for this particular style is attached; in this case, it is a design by Alastair Morton, from the late 1940s.*

Daphne Razzell (née Patten)

Ivy Mill No. 400

London Ref No. 803.
12. 14. 16.

white piqué

pockets

Cloth No. 16774.

1.24 *Style 803, with a Graham Sutherland fabric design.*
Daphne Razzell (née Patten)

y Mill No. 173. London Ref No. 540

Cloth No. 16364

1.25 *Style 540 with a dark cotton print reserved exclusively for Liberty, 1950.*
Daphne Razzell (née Patten)

1.26 *James Cleveland Belle, 1946.*
Design Council/University of Brighton
Design Archives
VADS: DCAA0354

a model from one of the fashion shows held at Hanover Square and having two or three fittings and sometimes slight alterations to the style. Apart from the occasional one-off garment, this was probably as close as Horrockses Fashions came to haute couture.

James Cleveland Belle

On 29 November 1948, Leslie Brown, Horrockses Fashions' design director, died suddenly at Hanover Square. The company had been operating for only two years and his premature death in his 40s was a shock to everyone. James Cleveland Belle (1.26), who had been appointed as a consultant in February 1948, with an annual fee of £1000, eventually took over the helm.[21] The groundwork had been put in place by Brown, but it was Belle's involvement with Horrockses Fashions that was to push its name to the forefront of progressive ready-to-wear design and the use of avant-garde fabrics. Belle had begun his career in retail. In the 1930s he had been a buyer at Bon Marché in Liverpool, but he is probably best known for his role as the first director of the Cotton Board's Colour, Design and Style

Centre (CDSC) in Manchester from 1940 to 1950. It was such experience that helped to boost Horrockses Fashions' growing reputation. Belle had been responsible for organizing a number of exhibitions at the CDSC, with the aim of raising the status of cotton as a fashion fabric. He was involved in the formation of the Incorporated Society of London Fashion Designers in 1942 and was largely responsible for organizing the textile and fashion content of the *Britain Can Make It* exhibition at the Victoria and Albert Museum in 1946.[22]

Belle's experience and energy in promoting cotton at the CDSC and his passion for good design all benefited Horrockses. His contribution was appreciated by the parent company and he became a director of several of the firm's subsidiaries. Although Alastair Morton had been supplying the firm with fabric designs since 1947 (1.27, 1.28), it was Belle who brought in several artists who he had worked with on exhibitions at the CDSC, including Graham Sutherland and John Farleigh. He made regular visits to the diploma shows of textile students, which resulted in the appointments of Joyce Badrocke as an in-house designer and Pat Albeck as a home-based salaried designer (see Chapter 2).

1.27 *A Horrockses Fashions'*
sunsuit, in a fabric by
Alastair Morton, 1948.
Courtesy of the Harris Museum
and Art Gallery, Preston:
PRSMG: 2003.83
Photographed by Norwyn Ltd

1.28 *A cotton dress from 1949,*
commissioned by the Calico
Printers Association in a 1947
fabric designed by Alastair Morton.
© Manchester City Galleries: CPA33

1.29 The Horrockses Fashions'
team in the salon at 15 St George
Street, Hanover Square, early
1950s. From left to right:
James Cleveland Belle, Marta Pirn,
Betty Newmarch, John Tullis,
Kathleen Molyneux (seated),
Marjorie Ritson, Ken Lusty.
AAD/1995/16/2/4

As design director of Horrockses Fashions, Belle worked very closely with Kurt Lowit, a textile chemist who came to Britain in 1939 from Czechoslovakia. Lowit was based at Ivy Mill, where he was responsible for engaging printers, for coordinating the translation of fabric designs for printing, and for the quality control of fabrics. He travelled to London frequently where he worked closely with Belle and the fashion designers in London, assisted in his tasks by Stephanie Godfrey.

In 1950, Horrockses Fashions decided to boost its couture credentials by employing a third fashion designer. The director's report of 1949 notes that the firm was doing well, but the appointment of John Tullis, whose background was in couture, was probably prompted by increasing competition in the industry, as new clothing producers entered the market after the end of consumer rationing in March 1949. Tullis was born in South Africa and was 28 when he joined Horrockses having learned his trade from his mother's cousin, Captain Edward Molyneux, in Paris. He was probably introduced to Horrockses by Kathleen Hope Lumley (née Molyneux), Edward Molyneux's sister. She had been working for Horrockses since 1949 as directrice, and looked after publicity following the death of Jane Edwardes (1.29). Known to everyone as 'Auntie Kathleen', she operated as a kind of 'figurehead' and, according to an employee of the firm, she knew everyone – from royalty and ladies-in-waiting downwards – and was instrumental in securing a number of well-known clients.[23] Although Horrockses Fashions never traded on an individual

stylist's name, Tullis was a strategic appointment and was largely, though not exclusively, responsible for the design of prestige garments. When Tullis's designs were produced in quantity at Ivy Mill, there were often complaints from machinists about the complexity of his designs.[24] His appointment reflects the firm's determination, under the leadership of Belle, to advance its high fashion credentials, but also highlights the continuing problem of balancing mass production and high fashion.

Seasons, styles and quantities

Across the industry, the production year was divided into two seasons. The main production cycles typically ran from November to April for the Spring/Summer collections, with shows taking place in May (or with predominantly cotton collections this could extend into June). Production took place from June to September for the Autumn/Winter collections, with shows taking place in October. Sometimes Horrockses Fashions would produce an extra range mid-season, with an accompanying show (as happened in February 1950), particularly if sales were slow, to encourage retailers to place orders.

Although many of those who worked for the company in the 1940s and 50s felt that Horrockses Fashions' styling was so particular that it did not follow Paris, evidence indicates otherwise. The company's records suggest that keeping in touch with Paris was very important; in 1949, Horrockses Fashions held off on a decision about the length of dresses in the Autumn/Winter range until the French collections were

1.30 Greta Hetherington purchased this dress in Blackpool in 1954. The arrangement of floral designs in stripes was a particularly popular treatment for Horrockses' cottons (see 4.1, p.142).
Courtesy of the Harris Museum and Art Gallery, Preston: PRSMG: 2000.302

1.31 An advertisement for an evening dress in 'Lansil' jersey.
Vogue, April 1953

Horrockses Fashions *in "Lansil" Jersey*

available. In the same year, there was a discussion about sending one of the Horrockses' fashion designers to see the Paris shows, although it is not clear if this actually happened. The company also considered applying to the Board of Trade for a permit to purchase garments from Paris. It is likely that this was pursued as, on a visit to Horrockses Fashions in the 1950s, actress Virginia McKenna recalls being shown a rack of clothes from the couture houses that Horrockses was selling off and she purchased a pale grey Balmain suit.[25] James Cleveland Belle noted in 1949 that, because of increasing competition, the company needed to have 'their finger on the pulse', as 'Numerous other firms were deliberately copying what was now known as Horrockses Fashions' style and it was, therefore,

necessary for us to maintain our lead this year by following closely Paris, London etc, fashion dictators and by adopting all the latest developments available to us.'[26] The company also kept a close eye on industry developments in the USA.

In terms of styling, Horrockses Fashions is probably best known for its crisp and simple cotton shirtwaisters made from colourful floral prints (1.30). However, it also produced glamorous evening dresses, made in cotton, jerseys (1.31), silks, and occasionally, in the second half of the 1950s, nylon. On average, the company produced between 150 and 160 styles per season made from 70 to 80 different fabric designs.[27] Summer dresses retailed at between £4 and £7 in the early 1950s, evening dresses between £7 and £16, and a housecoat sold for

1.32 *An early example of a*
Horrockses Fashions' housecoat,
1947.
Vogue, May 1947

1.33 *The interior of Tootal's*
Manchester factory in 1955.
Photograph by Charles Hewitt,
Getty Images, Hulton Archive

between £6 and £9 (1.32). In terms of quantities of dresses made to each style, this varied depending on the complexity of the style. In 1951, it was noted that '…the minimum of garments sold of any good print should be 1500 and that at least 1000 garments made to any one style was the lowest figure that could be practically accepted'.[28] However, in order to avoid the problem of mass production resulting in the possibility that 'the frocks would become "common"',[29] the company maintained a varied approach to production scale, with more complicated styles limited in quantities and some prestige lines produced in small numbers. Although production planning was crucial, a proportion of the season's range was improvised to enable a swift response to changing trends. The schedule in Table 1 gives the costings for a fairly typical collection for the company, divided into Utility and non-Utility production, and illustrates the scale of the company's operation. The total production for that collection was 159,822 garments (representing a value of £482,349), set against target sales of 178,100 at a value of £494,012.[30] Interestingly, there were orders for 187,228 garments, which illustrates the common practice within the

industry of 'overselling', whereby companies accepted more orders than they could supply. The assumption was that a number of customers would cancel and overselling would help protect the company from having unsold stock at the end of the season. Belle assured colleagues 'that to be successful in the fashion business and to become a first class dress firm one must accept the principle of overselling.'[31]

Manufacture

Like most firms producing model and medium quality ready-made women's wear, Horrockses Fashions operated the 'making-through' system at both its factories, whereby individual skilled machinists worked on a complete garment (1.33). This was favoured over the sectional system, where machinists worked on parts of garments depending on their skill level. The sectional system was increasingly favoured in the post-war industry, especially for lower, medium and cheap fashions. It helped to speed up production and, at a time when there was a shortage of skilled machinists, it allowed skilled staff to be used more effectively on the complicated sections of

STYLE NUMBER	DESCRIPTION	WHERE MADE	CLOTH QUALITY	CLOTH COST PER YARD	TOTAL FACTORY COST PER GARMENT (£)	TOTAL COST PER GARMENT (£)	SELLING PRICE(£)	PROFIT PER GARMENT(£)	PROFIT AS A % OF COST PRICE	PROFIT AS A % OF SELLING PRICE
UTILITY										
15	Cotton Dress	Ivy Mill	DGS503	50¼	40s.9d.	49s.4d.	48s.6d.	10d.	–	–
80	Cotton Dress	Ivy Mill	DGS503	44¾	33s.10d.	42s.1d.	48s.6d.	6s.5d.	15½%	13¼%
128	Cotton Dress	Ivy Mill	8054/1	79	48s.8d.	60s.	64s.4d.	4s.4d.	7%	6¾%
134	Cotton Sundress/Stole	Ivy Mill	DGS503	45	39s.4d.	46s.10d.	48s.6d.	1s.8d.	3½%	3%
190	Cotton Dress	Almo Gowns	DGS525	62½	37s.2d.	48s.3d.	53s.9d.	5s.6d.	11½%	10¼%
NON-UTILITY										
36	Cotton Dress	Ivy Mill	DGS524	97	67s.2d.	84s.9d.	105s.	20s.3d.	24%	19%
38	Cotton Dress	Ivy Mill	DGS503	52¼	47s.	58s.9d.	69s.9d.	10s.9d.	18¼%	15½%
58	Cotton Dress	Ivy Mill	F284	79	67s.3d.	83s.4d.	94s.6d.	11s.2d.	13½%	11¾%
73	Cotton Sundress	Ivy Mill	DGS503	52⅛	44s.6d.	56s.2d.	69s.6d.	13s.4d.	23¾%	19%
92	Cotton Evening Dress	Ivy Mill	DGS503	47	54s.9d.	68s.10d.	84s.	15s.2d.	22%	18%
125	Cotton Evening Dress	Ivy Mill	DGS525	61½	82s.9d.	102s.5d.	115s.6d.	13s.	12¾%	11¼%
135	Jersey Sundress/Bolero	Ivy Mill	R338H	56	68s.9d.	86s.4d.	105s.	18s.8d.	21¾%	17¾%
159	Evening Dress	Ivy Mill	Swiss	10/10	147s.6d.	187s.6d.	241s.6d.	54s.	28¾%	22½%
161	Evening Dress	Ivy Mill	DGS525	61½	74s.3d.	95s.7d.	115s.6d.	19s.11d.	20¾%	17¼%
163	Cotton Evening Dress	W.H. Cliffe	DGS503	51⅞	55s.2d.	69s.3d.	84s.	14s.9d.	21%	17½%
164	Cotton Evening Dress	Ivy Mill	DGS533	106½	106s.9d.	133s.4d.	157s.6d.	24s.2d.	18%	15½%
202	Evening Dress	Ivy Mill	DGS525	61½	84s.9d.	106s.6d.	130s.	23s.6d.	22%	18%

garments, leaving unskilled staff for simpler processes. Because of the wide range of styles produced in relatively small numbers in the model and medium quality end of production, the making-through system was retained by many manufacturers. Despite this, in 1951, after a time-and-motion study, Horrockses Fashions decided to change to a sectional system.[32] However, it quickly reverted back to the making-through system, which it felt was more suited to the fashionable garments it produced. It was also influenced by complaints from its machinists who preferred the old system. The desire to increase efficiency at its mills and to improve the quality of production led Horrockses to monitor the latest technical developments in the USA. As a result, it invested in a levelling machine in 1949 (at a cost of £50), which measured and trimmed a hem in one action and ensured that the fashionable large circular skirts were finished properly.[33]

Although Horrockses had its own making-up factories in Manchester and Congleton, seasonal production meant that it often used 'cut-make-and-trim' (CMT) firms to fulfil orders. These companies operated as contractors for the supply of made-up garments and usually had no in-house design operation. Horrockses Fashions used several and their usefulness was commented on: 'Without support of CMT [it would be] impossible to attain the 1952 turnover of £1,000,000'.[34] CMT firms seemed to be particularly important for the making-up of non-cotton dresses. However, some quality control issues were experienced,

> although we have had instances of inferior workmanship from some of these firms,... We have been well satisfied, however, with two London firms and Valmain of Southport for the silks etc. and with Polikoff in particular for the corduroys, and if we are to continue using Sekers fabrics I am certain that CMT production is the best policy to adopt...[35]

Fashion shows

Regular fashion shows were held at Hanover Square (rather in the manner of a couture house), with the parent company vacating its showrooms to accommodate them. Here, buyers, the press and special customers would view the company's collections two or three times a year. Initially, they were compèred by Jane Edwardes, who looked after publicity with the help of an assistant, Mrs Weller. At other times, buyers were taken to the first floor where rails of dresses were on display. Marjorie Ritson was head of the showroom and was referred to as the *vendeuse* (an affectation borrowed from Parisian couture), and, although she was responsible for looking after the company's 'special' clients, her main task was to take care of the buyers, Horrockses' principal customers. Mildred Rackham worked with her in the showroom as a sales person.

Other personnel at Hanover Square included Ken Lusty, Horrockses sales and export manager, Terence Altham, assistant to James Cleveland Belle, and Doris Spriggs, who looked after trimmings. Altham joined the London office in the late 1940s from the parent company in Preston and, when Belle left in 1958, Altham became director of women's wear. During the 1950s, each fashion designer had an assistant. Daphne Patten joined the firm in 1946 from Bromley College of Art and was originally employed as a fashion illustrator. When John Tullis joined the firm in 1950, Patten became his assistant. Between 1953 and 1956, Gloria Smythe took over this role.[36] Tullis was extremely supportive and gave his assistants several opportunities to design. Wendy Jackson was Marta Pirn's assistant and Sylvia Paulson worked for Betty Newmarch.

Horrockses Fashions abroad

The parent company singled out Horrockses Fashions in a director's report in 1948 and noted,

1.34 *A poplin shirtwaister, Spring/ Summer 1956. The skirt is cut with a square peplum from which a full skirt falls in a host of unpressed pleats. Photograph by John French.*
AAD/16/1/14

1.35 *A surviving example of a poplin dress photographed by John French in 1.34, 1956.*
Courtesy of the Harris Museum and Art Gallery, Preston: PRSMG: 1999.562.3
Photograph by Norwyn Ltd

We are happy to report that all our subsidiary companies made profits during the year, and it is pleasing to record the progress made by Horrockses Fashions Ltd. The demand for our fashions during the year, both at home and abroad, has fully confirmed the views expressed on previous occasions that cotton is still the most popular material for ready-to-wear garments, tastefully designed and properly styled.[37]

The company's success prompted the expansion of operations abroad, with the granting of licences to sell Horrockses Fashions' products (manufactured in the UK) in a number of countries, including Australia and New Zealand. In 1951, Horrockses Fashions (Canada) was established as a joint venture between Horrockses, Crewdson & Co. and H.M. Marler, using styles originated at the London headquarters, but with manufacturing completed in Canada.[38] Initially, there was some conflict of interest with the parent company. Following the formation of the company, sales of Horrockses, Crewdson & Co. cloth fell as other Canadian clothing manufacturers considered the fashion venture a threat to their sales. Eventually (in 1955), it was decided to sell particular fabric designs exclusively to the fashion subsidiary and anything not used by them could be sold to other makers-up. But, by 1956, the subsidiary was experiencing difficulties due largely to customers' desire for American styling and lighter-weight fabrics, so manufacture in Canada was suspended.[39]

Competition

As Horrockses Fashions became established, complaints were voiced about the number of competitors who were copying its style. In January 1950, Belle grumbled that it was 'now meeting competition from Marchingtons, Tootals, Cyril Lord etc., and that it was advisable to include in our range a considerable variety of cotton dresses'.[40] The initial help the company had received from Olive O'Neill at Rose & Blairman had been reciprocated by Horrockses Fashions creating garments for the firm, but, by October 1949, the relationship encountered difficulties as it was noted that 'Rose & Blairman had now gone in for cotton dresses and were "lobbying" Horrockses Fashions' customers. They were working with Cyril Lord and March Mills and showing them our samples. They were holding their shows early and in opposition to Horrockses'.[41] Noting its appreciation of the help Olive O'Neill had provided in the past, it was decided to modify the arrangement and supply the firm with cloth only.

Balancing volume production and exclusive status

The first few years of Horrockses Fashions saw the firm establish its reputation as a manufacturer of good quality ready-made women's wear, with an energetic and well-connected design director in James Cleveland Belle, a talented team of fashion designers in London, an extensive source of good fabric designs and an assured supply of quality cotton. It had its own factories, a series of reliable CMT manufacturers and was making a profit. However, growing tensions within the company were emerging as a result of trying to marry its fundamental business (ready-to-wear) with the more prestigious activity of producing specials and styles for limited production (1.34). The major problems that it encountered delivering the Spring 1951 range, and the resulting response, were to prove a turning point for the company.

The key issue that Horrockses Fashions faced in 1951 was a range where the number of styles kept growing during the course of the season. The total number of styles for the whole of 1950 had been 242 and it had been agreed that the range for Spring 1951 should be somewhere in the region of 124 to 136 styles. However, the final total had been 269, with 34 of the styles selling less than 100 garments. This added to the workload of the sample machinists in London, who were required to make up two sample garments for every style, and led to late deliveries to retail customers. In the course of an investigation into the failures of the 1951 Spring range, an additional problem emerged. During March to June 1951, the London sample room also made 98 specials, with 27 in process. These involved two to three fittings for 52 people and, while it was acknowledged that 'all of whom were of great value to us for publicity reasons', it was realized that the sample room could not be distracted from the main business of the company. The other problem identified was the complicated nature of some of the designs received by Ivy Mill, which had resulted in machinists threatening to strike – such designs were more time-consuming to make and were affecting their earning capacity (1.35). Many of the designs received by the factory in Manchester from London required frequent modifications to make them suitable for volume production.[42]

This investigation highlighted a number of issues that faced a ready-to-wear firm such as Horrockses Fashions, who were producing in quantity but at the same time attempting to create an illusion of exclusivity (1.36). The success it was enjoying in 1950 was born on the back of juggling mass production and high-class special lines, but by 1951 it had got the balance wrong. This lead to a reassessment of what the company was about, resulting in more efficient operations for the next few years. It was acknowledged that the company

Horrockses

1.37 *A cotton shirtwaister, printed in a check pattern on white, in yellow, grey and green, 1950.*
© Manchester City Galleries: 1951.224

needed to continue producing garments essentially for publicity purposes, but that styles for volume production had to be a priority for the London sample room. Therefore, it decided to contract out the making of the former to CMT firms. The company resolved to improve communications between the fashion designers in London and the activities of Ivy Mill and to transfer the pattern grader, Jimmy Peters, to London so that he could advise the designers as to what was and was not possible in terms of effective factory production. In addition, it reduced the percentage of flexibility allowed on each range (i.e. the addition of styles as the season progressed) from 25 per cent to 10–15 per cent.

The Horrockses Fashions' enterprise was an ambitious, unusual and timely venture in the promotion of cotton cloth through the manufacture of fashionable ready-to-wear clothing, using distinctive fabric design, supported by carefully considered promotion (1.37). The profitable volume production of women's fashion was disguised by the company's development of a distinctive brand identity that emphasized the glamour and exclusivity of the product. The negotiation of a successful balance between these two apparently divergent strategies led Horrockses Fashions to become one of the most sought-after ready-to-wear brands of the 1940s and 1950s and confirmed a newspaper's view that the company was enabling women 'to buy clothes with the Bond Street cachet at average purse prices'.[43]

Chapter 2
'In Fine Cotton':
Fabric and Fashion

The raw materials of fashion

Textiles were Horrockses Fashions' *raison d'être*. The parent company's intention to boost sales of its own cotton through this venture meant that concentration on pattern design, quality of fabric and standards of printing was paramount and was a key reason why Horrockses was so successful during the 1940s and '50s. Designs on fabric remained exclusive to the label, partly in an attempt to enhance the cachet of the brand, but also to prevent accusations of competition from clothing manufacturers who were regular customers of Horrockses, Crewdson & Co.'s piece goods. Horrockses Fashions' cotton cloth was praised by fashion commentators and consumers alike, with prints commended for their bright and fresh colours and patterns. A deliberate strategy was developed to employ fabrics to enhance the perceived exclusivity of the brand, by purchasing some designs from artist-designers and using several different textile patterns for one dress style (2.1).

According to Audrey Withers, 'To a designer, fabrics are the raw material of his craft… It is the fabric that determines the character of the dress – by its stiffness or suppleness, its draping or pleating qualities, its capacity for taking crisp pleats or fine tucks'.[1] This comment illustrates the significance of fabric to the fashion designer. It is surprising, therefore, to find a dearth of information on fashion fabrics, particularly when compared to the extensive literature available on the resulting clothes. Lesley Miller's essay on the relationship of the textile manufacturer to haute couture is an important contribution,[2] as is Lou Taylor's essay on the semiotic qualities of fashion fabrics.[3] The monograph by Valerie Mendes and Frances Hinchcliffe on

Ascher, the British-based producer and converter of fashion fabrics, provides an insight into the activities of a company working closely with the couture sector of the industry. However, there is little information relating to how a ready-to-wear manufacturer ensured that, in addition to producing clothes that followed Parisian styling, its products were up-to-the-minute in terms of fabric type, colour and pattern [4].

Designing fabric patterns for clothing required an appreciation of the human form, as the final fabric would be cut and constructed to create a three-dimensional product. The pattern designer needed to consider the scale of their design and the fact that the cloth might be draped, folded or pleated in the final garment. For a dress designer, a fabric could provide the inspiration for their design, and at the level of haute couture a new fabric or pattern might be designed to meet the specific requirements of a designer. Apart from a few exceptions, most ready-to-wear firms relied for their fabrics on merchant converters who sourced the design and arranged for cloth to be finished. The clothing manufacturer usually then purchased in bulk from already printed stock. A small number of textile companies developed ready-to-wear collections in order to utilize and promote their own fabric – Horrockses and Tootal are examples of such practice. It was essential for a ready-to-wear manufacturer producing garments with a strong fashion appeal to ensure that the fabrics it chose would enhance the styling of a garment and compliment seasonal trends. Fabric had to be sourced and ordered in sufficient quantities and in time, so that orders would be available when the collections were shown to retail buyers. Since Horrockses Fashions used cloth from the parent

'In Fine Cotton':
Fabric and Fashion

2.2 *A 1930s advertisement for Horrockses' dress fabrics.*
Film Fashionland, December 1934

2.3 *A sundress with bolero jacket in a fabric designed by Alastair Morton, early 1950s.*
Courtesy of the Harris Museum
and Art Gallery, Preston:
PRSMG: 2000.308

PARTY-FROCK FABRICS

Do you want your party frock in the grand manner? Copy the lady in the fashion-able tunic dress and choose Horrockses FORELLA CREPE in a delightful oriental two colour printed design. The lady in the hat picks SYLVAN CREPE for her chic afternoon dress and uses the new two colour contrast for belt and collar. The small girl with the teddy-bear is enchanting in Horrockses NINON, a printed fabric in lovely clear colours. And for the not-so-small girl the choice is Horrockses FASHION CREPE, in a gay plaid print. SYLVAN CREPE is usually retailed at 3/11d. a yard. FASHION CREPE, FORELLA and NINON at 2/11d. These are but four from our wide range of dress materials. There is a Horrockses Fabric suited to every hour of the day or night.

HORROCKSES

HORROCKSES, CREWDSON & CO. LTD., 107, PICCADILLY, MANCHESTER

company, originated or bought in its own fabric designs and organized printing, it was at an advantage compared to many of its competitors. If planned carefully, it could minimize the time it took between design of fabric and manufacture of garment (2.3).

Impact of the Second World War on fashion textiles
The pre-war fashion industry was dominated by the use of rayon, and manufacturers of the fibre benefited from a level of protection that had resulted in an expansion in production, with many cotton mills converted to rayon production. Wray asserts that the fibre was better suited for the factory production of clothing than the available cotton and that the resulting reasonably priced garments 'encouraged consumers to prefer ready-made dresses'.[5] Like all raw materials, cloth was controlled during the war, ensuring supplies of cloth at restricted prices to designated manufacturers. When the cloth allocation system ended in 1946, firms who had previously received regular cloth supplies were now competing for them. The end of rationing in 1949 and the entry into the market of new clothing producers created further competition.

Fortunately, Horrockses Fashions had the advantage of a ready supply of cotton cloth from the parent company. The other effect of war-time restriction was the exclusion of new man-made fibres from the Utility Scheme, which delayed their take up by clothing manufacturers until the Scheme ended in 1952.[6]

Cotton fashions
Horrockses, Crewdson & Co. had been selling cotton-based fashion fabrics to the home dressmaking market throughout the twentieth century, so it had enough experience in the field to realize that the success of a fashion label was partly dependent on using the right cloth with the appropriate design. The company's Preston mill had its own design studio producing shirtings, pyjama patterns, and designs for dress, tie and furnishing fabrics. Advertisements for the reasonably priced dress materials regularly appeared in women's magazines in the 1920s and '30s (2.2). The firm supplied grey cloth and some finished fabric to other women's wear wholesalers, including, for example, Grafton House and Rose & Blairman.

2.4 Screen-printed cotton dress
fabric from 1933 by
D. Marshall & Co Ltd.
V&A: T.426-1933

2.5 A floral stripe has been chosen
by the fashion designer for this
summer dress. The sketch indicates
to the factory how the stripe
should be configured.
Daphne Razzell (née Patten)

Cotton

Before the Second World War, cotton's reputation as a fashion fabric was low and it was associated with cheap, practical clothing, hardwearing sheets and children's wear. A so-called 'washing frock' would retail at 5 shillings, whereas a rayon garment, perceived as more modern and fashionable, was at least double.[7] Designs on cotton tended to be small geometric or floral patterns and were regarded as inferior to the designs found on silk (2.4). But the 1940s and '50s saw the ascendancy of cotton and, of all the ready-to-wear manufacturers, it was probably Horrockses Fashions that did more than any other to elevate its status as a fashion fabric, by combining well-styled garments, in bright, clear prints on good quality cloth (2.5). When it launched its first collection in 1946, reviews emphasized the company's glamorization of the fibre and the fact that designs were 'equal to those usually associated with printed silks and rayons'.[8] Commenting on Horrockses Fashions' first collection, the *Imperial Review* mentioned that 'Previously cotton was either very bold and vivid in design and colouring, or was in small geometrical or floral designs, associated with children's wear. The

use of "silk" designs, combined with the couturiers' art, produced clothes of an excellence never before seen in cotton'.[9]

Horrockses Fashions' garments were made from the parent company's high quality cotton sheeting. The most commonly used quality was known as 'DGS503', which was exclusive to the Horrockses Fashions' label. Qualities such as the lighter 'DGS501' and 'DGS104' were used but could also be purchased by other companies. The sheeting was robust yet soft to the touch and draped well; it did not shrink and could withstand frequent washing. Horrockses Fashions' cottons were treated to maintain a crisp finish, and dyeing and printing were of a standard that meant colours were fast. The impetus behind the launch of Horrockses Fashions was ultimately the sale of the parent company's cotton cloth, but, in addition, the venture was a response by the industry to promote cotton generally, with the establishment of the Cotton Board by an Act of Parliament in 1940. Initially known as the Cotton Industry Board, the Manchester-based organization's prime aim was to fulfil the need for a central body to represent the cotton industry. Financed by a levy on manufacturers, to

Ivy Mill No. 411.

- blue stripe

blue stripe

London Ref. No. 828.

12. 14. 16.

Cloth No. 16939.

2.6 *A Colour, Design and Style Centre exhibition, Manchester, 1952.*
Photograph by John McCormack of Elsam, Mann & Cooper, Manchester, Ltd. Metropolitan University, Special Collections [Cotton Board, Colour, Design and Style Centre archive]

2.7 *A view of the upstairs exhibition space at the Colour, Design and Style Centre, Manchester, 1952.*
Photograph by John McCormack of Elsam, Mann & Cooper, Manchester, Ltd. Metropolitan University, Special Collections [Cotton Board, Colour, Design and Style Centre archive]

begin with it was created to perform functions relating to the war, but it also worked towards the re-establishment of the industry in peacetime. Its purpose was to extend export trade, promote research and experimentation within the industry, to collect and disseminate relevant statistics and to conduct negotiations. It was important to raise the status of cotton as a fashion fabric, in order to help expand the market for cotton cloth, and the creation of Horrockses Fashions was a perfect expression of that aspiration.

The Colour, Design and Style Centre (CDSC) was the Board's public face (2.7). Its first director was James Cleveland Belle, who was eventually to become the design director of Horrockses Fashions. Belle was particularly adept at

encouraging young fabric designers and his experience in fashion retail and in the promotion of cotton meant he was a valuable asset to Horrockses. The intention of the CDSC, also based in Manchester, was to raise standards in design on cotton by bringing together fabric designers and manufacturers. It did this by organizing numerous exhibitions, supported by the central fund of the Cotton Board (between 1940 and 1956 more than 80 exhibitions were organized) (2.6). It held a comprehensive library and a register of textile designers and undertook market research.[10] In order to try to promote the use of cotton as a fashion fabric, the Board and the Centre realized the value of encouraging its use by British-based couturiers, who were experiencing problems obtaining fabrics from overseas during

2.8 *A display of fabrics and fashions at the Cotton Board's Colour, Design and Style Centre, Manchester, including dresses by Horrockses Fashions, 1951.*
Photograph by John McCormack of Elsam, Mann & Cooper, Manchester, Ltd. Metropolitan University, Special Collections [Cotton Board, Colour, Design and Style Centre archive]

the war. The Centre assisted the newly formed Incorporated Society of London Fashion Designers by advising on suitable fabrics, liaising with converters and arranging for special fabrics to be produced for its export collection for a tour of South America in 1941. It was felt that the involvement of couturiers resulted in many wholesale houses turning to cotton as a suitable fabric for fashion (2.8). This was confirmed at the Cotton Board's fashion show, *Cotton in Fashion 1951*, held at the Dorchester Hotel during London Fashion Fortnight (at the end of May and beginning of June). A number of leading British couturiers showed their cotton creations, for example, Victor Stiebel and Michael Sherard, but they were outnumbered by the products of ready-to-wear manufacturers, which included

Horrockses Fashions, Susan Small and Frederick Starke.[11] Donald Tomlinson of the CDSC noted that 'the success of wholesale cotton dresses has been so remarkable that some couturiers admit that their customers are well satisfied with the best products of the wholesale industry'.[12]

The take up of cotton in the late 1940s was in part due to the introduction of Christian Dior's 'Corolle' line, launched in 1947 and later christened the 'New Look' by the press. The New Look was the perfect style for cotton (2.9). The softly tailored shoulders, nipped-in waists and voluminous skirts responded wonderfully to the new qualities of cool, crisp cottons now available and the copious yards of fabric required were a bonus to the cotton industry. Although

2.9 *A cotton sundress in an African print, 1950.*

Daphne Razzell (née Patten)

2.11 *Horrockses Fashions made several wedding dresses for staff working in George Street. Daphne Patten wore a dress designed by Marta Pirn when she married Arthur Razzell in 1950. The fabric, a cotton broderie anglaise, was imported from Switzerland.*
Daphne Razzell (née Patten)

2.10 *A cotton poplin dress, using contrasting coloured fabrics to emphasize complex cutting.*
Photograph by John French.
AAD/1995/16/3/16

cotton had been used to a limited extent in Parisian couture in the 1930s, it was not until the late 1940s that it began to be taken seriously by couturiers. For example, Elsa Schiaparelli included a cotton evening dress in a collection of 1947 and Dior was persuaded to use it by the fabric converter Ascher the following year.[13] Horrockses Fashions quickly took up the style, although with a less extravagant use of fabric; for mass-produced dresses, an average of five to six yards of fabric was used. By the mid-1950s, cotton was the preferred fabric for a large proportion of ready-to-wear production, as well as being seen in couture collections; frequently, the word 'glamour' was used to describe the fabrics. The majority of cotton fabric was provided by Horrockses, Crewdson & Co.

but it also used cotton poplins for more expensive garments (2.10), particularly evening wear, which was bought in from Ashtons and from Holdens, while cotton broderie anglaise was imported from St Gallen, Switzerland (2.11).

Use of non-cotton fabrics

Although Horrockses Fashions is associated primarily with cotton, it used a number of other fabrics in order to stay competitive and to help keep its making-up units in work throughout the year. To that end, it added styles in fabrics suitable for Autumn/Winter, for example, wool and corduroy, and these were purchased from outside the Horrockses group. Rayon jersey appeared for the first time in 1947

Ivy Mill No.   London Ref. No. 737.

Cloth No. 16540.

2.12 *A sketch for a dress (style 737) with a printed rayon jersey sample attached.*
Daphne Razzell (née Patten)

2.13 *A Horrockses Fashions' advertisement for a printed rayon evening dress.*
Vogue, May 1951

and was used for a variety of styles. Initially, Horrockses purchased the fabric from the Lancaster firm, Lansil Limited, and later from Jerseycraft in Huddersfield. While it would sometimes use plain jersey, it was more common for the company to arrange for the fabric to be printed using its own designs (2.12). Jersey featured regularly in Horrockses collections and it was noted that it was 'very popular with fashionable London shops.'[14] The nature of the cloth meant that the styles produced were quite different from its cotton dresses, as they tended to rely on moulding and draping the cloth rather than on tailoring (2.13). Although jersey was popular, Horrockses Fashions was cautious about expanding production of these dresses. Several competitors, including wholesale couturiers Roecliffe & Chapman, had increased the proportion of rayon jersey dresses that they produced. In 1949, 50 per cent of Roecliffe & Chapman's production was devoted to jersey and had been extremely well received by the press (30 per cent was devoted to cotton and the remainder to silk). James Cleveland Belle was recorded as feeling that the move by other firms towards jersey at cotton's expense was a mistake.[15] By comparison, Horrockses maintained jersey dresses at around 13 per cent, with the bulk of its production (about 85 per cent) reserved for cotton. The company believed that as the name Horrockses was synonymous with cotton it was this that should represent the majority of its output.

2.14 *Barbara Goalen wearing a Horrockses Fashions' dress in an advertisement for Sekers' nylon. The dress was designed by Daphne Razzell (née Patten).* Vogue, *March 1953.*

2.15 *An advertisement for Sekers' nylon featuring Horrockses Fashions.* Vogue, *October 1957*

A small number of non-cottons featured in the Spring/Summer collections, especially silk, which was still the favoured fabric of couture designers. Horrockses used silk particularly for its evening wear, where nylon was also occasionally seen (2.15). In 1952, the *Sunday Times* announced that 'Many women will be glad to know that Horrockses are now making dresses for the autumn and winter. Beautifully cut, in Sekers' tweed-like rayons and silks, wool-jersey, nylon and corduroy, they look much more expensive than they are. Already they are proving a great success with the buyers.'[16] Sekers (West Cumberland Silk Mills) was a key supplier of Horrockses' non-cottons. Founded by Hungarian émigré Nicholas Sekers (Miki) in a government development area in Whitehaven, Cumbria, the company produced fashion fabrics that were seen regularly on the Paris catwalks (2.14).

Fabric Design
The textile industry has always been a voracious consumer of designs. In 1937, Nikolaus Pevsner commented that one unnamed mass producer of dress fabrics used approximately 800 designs a year,[17] and it is clear from the business records of Horrockses Fashions and interviews with its employees that the acquisition of good designs was considered a priority. When asked to comment on what he felt were the main elements in a successful fashion business, James Cleveland Belle replied 'that there was no doubt that the following factors in the order stated were vitally important. 1. Colour and design. 2. The cut of the dress. 3. The quality', going on to comment 'that if we could get the right colours (i.e. bright colours) we could get away with "murder" in regard to the making of the dresses'.[18]

Horrockses Fashions' first collection included striped cottons, florals, a design of large feathers, a palm tree pattern and a West African print. Designs were initially provided by the parent company and were either bought in or originated by its own design studio in Preston. Kurt Lowit was employed as the technical adviser of colour and fabric design; he was responsible for directing the various printers and finishers contracted by Horrockses Fashions. He worked very closely with Horrockses Fashions' first design director, Leslie Brown,

2.16 *An advertisement for Sambo Fashions, one of Horrockses Fashions' competitors.*
The Ambassador, no.11, 1953

2.17 *An abstract pattern designed by Joyce Badrocke.*
AAD/2009/4

and later with James Cleveland Belle, and was involved in the purchase of suitable fabric designs and the appointment of fabric designers.

Floral patterns were the mainstay of Horrockses Fashions, with frequent complaints about shortages of good examples. They were treated in many ways, from quite natural interpretations to highly stylized treatments. Often they were arranged in stripes (known as *bayadere*) that came to be so closely associated with Horrockses Fashions and were often imitated by its competitors, as frequent comments in its business records attest (2.16). However, in order to vary its 'handwriting' and keep the brand fresh, it adopted patterns that relied on other idioms, including geometry and abstraction (2.17). The importance of the fabric pattern is highlighted in a comment from a Horrockses Fashions'

Australian licensee, California Productions in Sydney, who complained about having to place orders before seeing a sample, 'I know you will readily appreciate what I mean when I say that the design of the fabric and the style of the garment are so much related that any orders placed prior to receiving the sample garments are almost in the nature of a gamble.'[19]

Horrockses had a varied approach to the acquisition of patterns, with designs provided by in-house employees, contracted individuals or bought in from design studios, freelance fabric designers and occasionally from well-known artists. One of the first fabric designers associated with the firm was Marny Tittle; she began her career working for Horrockses, Crewdson & Co. in the Preston design studio in 1943 (2.18). There she designed the patriotic repeating pattern of a map of the British Isles interspersed with lines from Shakespeare,

2.18 The design studio in Horrockses, Crewdson & Co.'s
Preston factory. Marny Tittle (second from the right) began
her career here in 1943, before moving to Ivy
Mill, Manchester in the late 1940s.

Marny Shorrocks (née Tickle)

2.19 Marny Tittle's fabric design was used for several styles in Horrockses Fashions' first collection in 1946.
AAD/1995/16/12/1

which was used in the very first collection (2.19). In the late 1940s, she went on to work full time for Horrockses Fashions at Ivy Mill. However, Horrockses purchased the majority of designs from freelancers and design studios. Marny Tittle recalls accompanying Leslie Brown, Betty Newmarch, Kurt Lowit and Victoria Higgs (head of the Preston design studio) on a trip to Paris in 1946, their main task being the purchase of fabric designs. It was one of Tittle's tasks to prepare these designs (usually purchased as a sketch) for printing, working on scale, putting them into repeat and producing several colourways (this was the standard practice within the industry). Factory fabric designers such as Tittle often entered industry straight from school and supplemented their education at the local technical college. Tittle attended night school at the Harris Institute, Preston, where she gained a City and Guilds in Cotton Manufacture (Weaving) in 1948. This meant that she was adept at understanding the technical aspects of fabric production and finishing. In the early 1950s, she attended Manchester School of Art on a day release scheme.[20]

Design education

The 1940s and '50s saw a number of developments in the training of fabric designers. Provincial colleges, particularly in the north-west, provided local industry with designers who were required to be technically proficient rather than have artistic flair. They often spent most of their careers preparing the designs of freelancers and studios for production.

Criticized in the 1930s for its emphasis on fine art, the Royal College of Art (RCA) underwent a radical overhaul in 1948 under its new principal Professor Robin Darwin. The original School of Design was divided into specialist schools that included textile design (print and weave) and fashion. The aim was to equip designers with the skills needed to enter industry, while at the same time developing their creative talents. Students received a Des RCA after having spent a year working in industry. Most students who attended had already completed more general art and design courses at art schools. The RCA provided a particularly useful training ground for Horrockses Fashions' fabric designers. Joyce Badrocke (2.20) and her twin sister, Joan were both

2.20 Joyce Badrocke (in sunglasses) with a friend, both wearing Horrockses' dresses.
Joyce Badrocke

2.21 This organdie length was designed and printed by Joyce Badrocke for her Royal College of Art diploma show in 1950. It was bought by James Cleveland Belle for Horrockses Fashions and resulted in Badrocke being employed by the firm as their in-house fabric designer.
AAD/2009/4

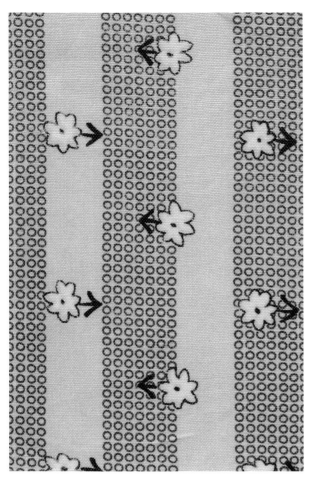

2.23 The background stripe of this daisy pattern was created by Joyce Badrocke by repeating the '0' numeral on a typewriter.
AAD/2009/4

2.24 A design by Joyce Badrocke. A dress in a blue version of this pattern was chosen by Queen Elizabeth II for her 1953–4 tour of New Zealand.
AAD/2009/4

awarded scholarships to attend the College after gaining their National Diplomas in Design from Worthing School of Art in 1947 and Joyce went on to work for Horrockses Fashions from 1950 to 1957. Joyce's talent was spotted by James Cleveland Belle at her 1950 diploma show, and he purchased a design from that show which was put into production (2.21, 2.22). The same year, he offered her a position at Horrockses Fashions' London headquarters. On starting with Horrockses, Joyce earned £5, which rose to £7 in 1955. She originated designs as well as preparing those

bought in for printing, while the designers based at Ivy Mill tended to be more technical, their main job being to prepare the designs for the printers. As a staff designer, Joyce was required to work in many styles during her seven years with Horrockses Fashions, from florals and geometrics (2.23, 2.24), to small novelty patterns for the Pirouette children's wear brand (2.25). She also produced several designs that referred to abstract expressionism. Of particular note is the design she refers to as 'inkspot', (2.26) where a splash of black is arranged over a coloured ground.[21]

2.25
*A fabric designed by Joyce Badrocke
for Horrockses Fashions' children's
range, Horrockses Pirouette.*
AAD/2009/4

2.26 *A fabric design by
Joyce Badrocke based
on an inkspot.*
AAD/2009/4

Horrockses Fashions
in Fine Cotton

"Evening News"

Ink Spots

What next? "Ink spots," spattered unevenly all over plain prints, are shown in day and evening dresses.

They spatter a very simple dance dress of white poplin, full-skirted and with a tiny bodice, its detachable fichu lined with black velvet.

There are black ink spots, too, on a day dress of tangerine poplin.

2.27 *An Alastair Morton fabric design, 1947.*
Christine Boydell

Alastair Morton

The question of sourcing good designs is a recurring topic of Horrockses Fashions' business records and in 1949 James Cleveland Belle complained that 'at the present time we are not overblessed in England with inspired designers'.[22] However, it was fortunate to have the services of Alastair Morton, who was a key figure in the company's early success (2.27). Morton was closely involved in his family's furnishing fabric firm, Morton Sundour, and specifically a branch of the firm, Edinburgh Weavers, described by Nikolaus Pevsner in 1936 as 'the most adventurous firm in the country'.[23] Morton had lectured many times on the subject of the fabric designer in industry and, unlike some, he did not consider designing for textiles to be a lowly subject, 'Dress designs and interior decoration are as genuine and important aspects of the cultured life of a country as are literature, music and art.'[24] After the Second World War, Morton continued as design director for Edinburgh Weavers on a half-time basis, allowing him to pursue other activities such as handloom weaving and designing fashion fabrics for Horrockses. Morton's status is reflected in the fact that from April 1947 he was paid a monthly retainer of £62.10s. In return, he was expected to provide at least 40 designs each year, which he supplied in repeat and in several colourways. (2.28)[25] These designs were characterized by their bright colours and loosely drawn flowers, often arranged in horizontal coloured stripes, which were to be widely imitated by Horrockses' rivals (2.29,

2.28 *A group of samples by
Alastair Morton. Unlike many
other fabric designers used by
Horrockses, Morton always
provided colourways and the design
in repeat. This design can be seen in
the skirt in 2.31*

*Reproduced by courtesy of Abbot Hall
Art Gallery, Kendal, Cumbria*

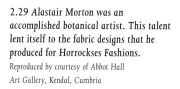

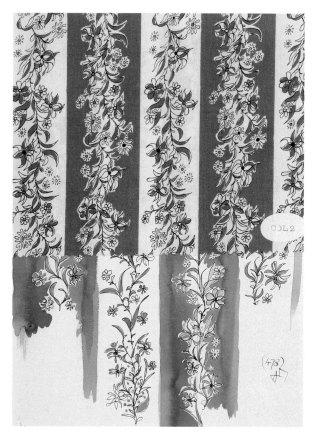

2.29 *Alastair Morton was an
accomplished botanical artist. This talent
lent itself to the fabric designs that he
produced for Horrockses Fashions.*

*Reproduced by courtesy of Abbot Hall
Art Gallery, Kendal, Cumbria*

2.30 *A very typical Alastair
Morton flower print.*

*Reproduced by courtesy of Abbot Hall
Art Gallery, Kendal, Cumbria*

2.30). *Fashions and Fabrics Overseas* concluded that 'they sold because they were fresh, different and excellently designed for their purpose'.[26] His prodigious output included small-scale patterns, such as a spot and stripe with a medallion containing a sketchy representation of a flower (2.33), and designs in a more abstract idiom, for example, incorporating a sunburst motif (2.32), or patterns derived from hypotrochoids (2.34).[27] Many of Morton's designs were used for Horrockses Fashions' children's wear range. The management of Horrockses Fashions agreed that Morton had played a crucial role in the company's initial success and 'undoubtedly set a fashion in Great Britain'.[28] The firm continued to use him into the 1950s, although in 1949

HORROCKSES, GREWDSON & CO. LTD.
PRESTON

2.31 *A dress with a full skirt in an Alastair Morton floral design c.1950. Colourway samples can be seen in 2.28.*
AAD/9/1/1979/3110-1

2.32 *A sample of a fabric by Alastair Morton in DGS503 quality cotton. See page 168.*
Reproduced by courtesy of Abbot Hall Art Gallery, Kendal, Cumbria

2.33 *A sketch of a sundress and bolero. The fabric attached is an Alastair Morton pattern.*
Daphne Razzell (née Patten)

y Mill No. 121

London Ref No. 537

12. 14. 16

Cloth No. 16162

2.34 *An Alastair Morton fabric design based on hypotrochoids.*
Reproduced by courtesy of Abbot Hall
Art Gallery, Kendal, Cumbria

2.35 *An advertisement for a poplin evening dress in a print designed by Margaret Meades, 1949.*
Vogue, April 1949

Harvey Nichols
of Knightsbridge

Summer evening dress in Horrockses poplin in a design exclusive to us. White ground only.
Hip sizes 36-42. (7 coupons) £10.18.0
Moderate Price Shop . . . first floor

some concern was expressed that its customers had 'seen too much of the Alastair Morton designs' and that it was striving to find a new fabric designer with a 'definite handwriting'.[29] In spite of this comment, the contract with Morton continued until 1955 when, due to increasing commitments at Edinburgh Weavers, he decided to end the arrangement, although he did express a desire to design for Horrockses from time to time.[30] A similar agreement operated for Margaret Meades, described as 'a young designer of printed fabrics whose fine drawing and individual style make her one of the most promising of a new generation of British textile artists.'[31] She studied at Manchester School of Art, where she was spotted by James Cleveland Belle when he was judging her diploma show. She was particularly adept at flower drawing using fine lines overlaid with brushstrokes of colour, which was ideally suited to the Horrockses Fashions style (2.35).

2.36 *A fabric design*
by Pat Albeck.
AAD /2004/9/70/3

2.37 *A pineapple and rose*
fabric design by Pat Albeck.
AAD/2004/9/73

2.38 *John Tullis asked Pat Albeck to produce a design for a fabric with a*
large-scale lobster. However, she did not feel that it worked on its own, so
added flowers and butterflies.
AAD/2004/9/74/2

Pat Albeck

On a visit to the RCA in 1952, Kurt Lowit and James Cleveland Belle discovered another talent, Pat Albeck. Albeck had attended Hull College of Art before moving to London. During her second year at the RCA, she was employed by Horrockses Fashions, spending alternate months designing fabrics for them and sometimes working at Ivy Mill. During this period, she sold designs to Tootal, Liberty and Ascher. When she graduated in 1953, Horrockses offered her a permanent position. Although she was a salaried employee, Albeck was based at home, with a starting wage of £12 per week. She worked directly with the fashion designers Marta Pirn, Betty Newmarch and John Tullis and was involved in the meetings that took place at Hanover Square with Belle, Lowit, Lowit's assistant Stephanie Godfrey and the fashion designers. It was in this collaborative context that decisions about the combination of style and textile design, as well as colour, were made. Albeck has described that when she designed it was always with a garment in mind (2.36, 2.37). She frequently worked closely with Tullis who was responsible for most of the prestige dresses and he would

Exclusive to
Bon Marché
in Liverpool
HORROCKSES *for Holidays Ahead !*

A glamorous sweep of crisp gay
cotton, buttoning from neck to hem.
Sky/rose; sky/pacific; lemon/orange;
rose/grey; lemon/grey.
Sizes 36-40 **4 gns.**

*You may order with
confidence by post.*

BON MARCHÉ · CHURCH STREET · LIVERPOOL 1

2.39 This cocktail dress was
probably designed by John Tullis.
The bodice and skirt were made
from related but different patterns,
known as 'unit' designs. Such a
practice was used for dresses where
quantities were limited.
Courtesy of the Harris Museum
and *Art Gallery*, Preston:
PRSMG: 2001.36

2.40 An advertisement for the
department store Bon Marché in
Liverpool featuring a 4 guinea
Horrockses' dress in a fabric
designed by Pat Albeck.
Vogue, April 1954

2.41 *A finely drawn rose pattern*
by Pat Albeck.
AAD/2004/9/71

often be quite specific about the type of fabric design that he wanted. For example, she produced a bold surreal lobster print for him in 1953 (2.38) and an extravagant design of peppers and sweetcorn in 1956. Unlike most of the patterns that Horrockses produced, these designs were conceived for a specific style of dress and were often used in designs where the bodice and skirt were made from related but different patterns (known as 'unit' designs). They were then printed up in limited quantities using the screen printing method (2.39). Although she designed some very recognizable Horrockses' *bayadere* floral striped designs (2.40), the majority of Albeck's work was quite different from Morton's, and varied from bold floral prints

2.42 *A fabric with a design for large-scale poppies from 1953, which was included in Pat Albeck's 1953 diploma show at the Royal College of Art.*
AAD/2004/9/83

2.43 *A grapevine pattern by Pat Albeck, 1953.*
AAD/2004/9/72/1

2.44 *A housecoat designed by Betty Newmarch in a Pat Albeck fabric. This was the first of Albeck's designs to be produced commercially. The same pattern was used for a dress and bolero outfit by Marta Pirn, 1953.*
The Ambassador, no.12, 1952

such as a dark pink poppy (2.42), to series of small-scale, finely drawn patterns inspired by Wedgwood ceramics (2.41, 2.43), and simplified floral forms that anticipated prints of the 1960s (2.44). She was also involved in an unusual venture translating into pattern the costume designs of the stage designer Sophie Fedorovitch for the operas *La Traviata* and *Orphée et Eurydice*.

These were sensitively interpreted to create unique dress fabrics (2.45).[32]

Artist-designers

A remit of the Colour, Design and Style Centre was to introduce artists and designers to the textile industry through exhibitions

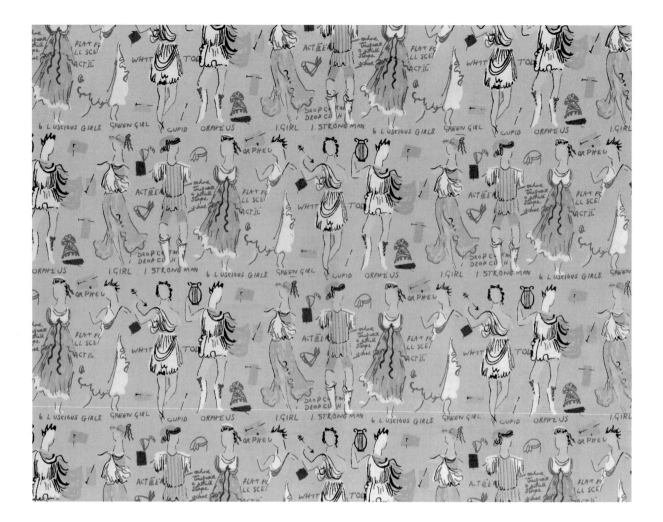

2.45 This is one of several fabric
designs by Pat Albeck from
costume designs for opera by
Sophie Fedorovitch: this one
is based on Orphée.
AAD/2004/9/88

at its Manchester headquarters. One such show focused on the work of a numbers of painters. *Design for Textiles by Fine Artists*, held in 1941, included work by Graham Sutherland, John Piper and Gerald Wilde. The idea of artist-designed textiles was not new. A number of initiatives before the Second World War had driven the idea that artists should play a central role in design for modern life. Paul Nash's block-printed fabrics for the workshop and gallery Modern Textiles in the 1920s are an example, and Alec Walker's Crystéde, a venture producing block-printed silks for the dress market, is another. The company Cresta, which developed out of the Crystéde enterprise, continued the practice of using the work of artists, such as Cedric Morris, Paul Nash and Patrick Heron. Larger manufacturers, including Edinburgh Weavers, Warner & Sons, David Whitehead and Donald Brothers, used artists for their furnishing fabrics.[33] The motivation behind such enterprises was twofold: on one level, companies employing the services of artists valued the publicity generated by the use of a painter's name in their promotion, while on a more ideological level, those involved had a commitment to the democratization of fine art through design and were committed to the reformist notion that such a direction might improve design and therefore people's lives. Horrockses Fashions rarely used an artist's name in consumer advertising, but the practice did result in exposure in the fashion and trade press and placed the company at the centre of progressive fabric design for fashion.

2.46 Detail from a screen-printed
rayon dress fabric designed
by Julian Trevelyan for
Ascher Ltd, 1946.
V&A: Circ.95B-1947

2.47 Detail from a cotton
shirtwaister dress made from
a fabric designed by
Graham Sutherland.
Target Gallery

The role of art in textiles increased during the 1940s and 1950s, with significant numbers of women wearing clothing made from fabrics whose patterns had been created by some of the most well-known artists of the day. Nikolaus Pevsner felt the timing was due to the fact that painting was developing a more abstract idiom, 'Problems of pure form and colour, that is of pattern, are the chief content of art... Now pattern is also what matters to the dress trade. So here the interests of the textile manufacturer and the modern artist meet'.[34] The practice was driven by the activities of the Colour, Design and Style Centre and by a number of individual companies committed to the dissemination of good design through mass-produced goods, including Horrockses Fashions.

In 1939, Lida and Zika Ascher, Czech émigrés, established a small textile business in London, and in the 1940s produced on cloth the designs of a number of leading British and French artists (2.46). As well as headscarves that almost worked as silk canvases, the company produced dress lengths with designs by Lida Ascher and commissioned work from a number of artists, including Henry Moore, Matisse, Paule Vézelay and Feliks Topolski, printed on cotton, rayon and silk. These were enthusiastically adopted by couture fashion and the success they achieved led the Aschers to undertake design and production for the mass market, under the name Bourec. Established in 1946, this division of the company supplied fabric to companies such as the ready-to-wear firms Sambo and Mattamac.[35]

2.48 *A cotton shirtwaister in a fabric designed by Graham Sutherland.* Horrockses Fashions purchased a number of designs from Sutherland in the late 1940s and early 1950s.

Always on the lookout for new approaches to pattern design, Horrockses Fashions also sought out artists for ideas for cloth. This method was largely instigated by James Cleveland Belle and he was responsible for introducing fabric designers to the company who were to help make Horrockses' output so distinctive and desirable. In 1949, Graham Sutherland was mentioned as a possible replacement for Alastair Morton and it was agreed he should be contacted to provide the company with 'design ideas', which would be prepared for printing by the firm's own staff designers.[36] He had previously worked for other textile firms including T.A. Wardle, Ascher, John Heathcoat and Warner & Sons. Belle commented that as Sutherland was now becoming a well-known artist his name would hopefully stimulate press interest in Horrockses' collections.[37] The firm used several designs by Sutherland in the late 1940s and early 1950s and these were not necessarily restricted to prestige lines and specials. Sutherland's work was used for a number of garment styles, including simple shirtwaisters and sundresses with bolero jackets, which were produced in quantity (2.48). The designs ranged from sculptural forms and abstract themes to bold floral designs, such as a rose pattern, a motif which he used regularly in his textile work (2.47).

In 1953, Horrockses Fashions developed a fabric design from a painting by Eduardo Paolozzi, which the company had purchased from the exhibition *Painting into Textiles*, held at the Institute of Contemporary Arts and sponsored by *The Ambassador* (the British export magazine). Hans and Elsbeth Juda (she used the pseudonym Jay for her work as a photographer), who ran the magazine, were key figures in the promotion of artist-designers in the textile industry. Artists were requested to submit paintings for the exhibition that were intended to inspire designs. It was felt that an artist's lack of knowledge of the technicalities of production would prove an asset rather than a problem, resulting in a greater freedom of expression. The outcome was an exciting display of paintings by 27 artists, together with contributions from a number of textile designers, including Pat Albeck. Many paintings were purchased by manufacturers: for example, Horrockses Fashions and Horrockses, Crewdson & Co. bought two works by William Gear and Horrockses Fashions bought a Paolozzi canvas which was translated almost exactly into a dramatic two-colour design on white cotton. (2.50, 2.51) A number of colourways were produced: a bright yellow and black on a white ground, and a lilac and black (2.49). A few of the artists involved in the show had designed for fabric before, such as Piper, Moore and Paolozzi, who at this time taught textile design at the Central School of Arts and Crafts.

It was through the Judas that Horrockses was introduced to Louis le Brocquy, an Irish painter who had designed tapestries for Edinburgh Tapestry Weavers in the 1940s. In 1955, he travelled to Spain with Elsbeth Juda. On their return, le Brocquy developed his sketches and Juda's photographs into a series of fabric designs for three manufacturers: David Whitehead, Sekers and Horrockses Fashions.[38] His brief was

2.49 *An alternative colourway
of Eduardo Paolozzi's 1953
fabric design.*
Jean Grinsted

2.50 *A strapless cotton cocktail dress with black poplin cummerbund in a fabric designed by Eduardo Paolozzi.*
The Ambassador, no.12, 1953

2.51 *A Horrockses Fashions' cocktail dress in a print based on an Eduardo Paolozzi painting, which featured in the Painting into Textiles exhibition held at the Institute of Contemporary Arts in 1953.*
Courtesy of the Harris Museum
and Art Gallery, Preston:
PRSMG: 2003.81
Photograph by Norwyn Ltd

1173075/2 — light ground.
1173075/1 — dark » Cummerband

2.52 *A page from Patricia Hunter's sketchbook 1955–6, showing a print designed by Louis le Brocquy, which was used in a dress worn by Princess Margaret.*
AAD/1995/16/5/1

2.53 *Princess Margaret is seen wearing a Horrockses' dress on her 1956 tour of Africa; the fabric design is by Louis le Brocquy.*
Rex Features

2.54 *A Horrockses Fashions' publicity still of a dress with a full skirt in an African print, 1950.*
Christine Boydell

completely open and he considered the end use of the designs for furnishing and fashion fabrics. He provided sketches for each company that were translated in-house and these were exhibited at the London gallery, Gimpel Fils. Like many artists involved in fabric design at the time, le Brocquy saw this activity as an extension of his role as a fine artist (2.52, 2.53).[39] This practice of collaboration between manufacturer and artist illustrated Horrockses Fashions' commitment to innovative textile design.

Freelancers and design studios

The work of staff designers and artists was outnumbered by the acquisition of large quantities of designs from outside the company, from freelancers and design studios (British, French and Italian). This allowed Horrockses to achieve what it described as 'a variety of handwriting'.[40] The commercial studios included the eminent Parisian firm, Suzanne Kientz and Lizzie Derrier, and Manchester-based studios such as Ivan de Coutére, Headon Designs, and Arthur Morris, who was known for his flower drawing. George Ainscow began his career specializing in 'African' patterns for dress, first with Headon Designs, one of the largest design studios in the country, and then with de Coutére (2.54). In 1950, Ainscow established his own studio and supplied designs for Horrockses, Crewdson & Co. and Horrockses Fashions, Tootal and Marchingtons.[41]

2.55 *Kurt Lowit, technical advisor of colour and fabric design. The woman is his assistant, Stephanie Godfrey.*
Maria Lowit

Pat Albeck recalled prices paid for designs at the time as: 10 guineas for a large croquis, 8 guineas for a small sketch, and 10 shillings for colourways.[42] The list of freelancers selling to Horrockses is long and their contribution to the dress industry has yet to receive adequate attention, but a few examples are: Sheila Chalmers, Brigette Dehnert, Joyce Fidler, Constance Green, Joyce Morgan, James Morris and Joyce Storey. In the late 1940s and early 1950s, Terence Conran sold about 20 designs to Horrockses (he was paid £25 for a design in repeat and £5 per colourway). His work had been seen by Belle at his exhibition at the Central School, where he was taught textile design by Eduardo Paolozzi. Conran was briefed by Belle and expected to design in 'a Horrockses style', and he recalls that colour was considered particularly important.[43] Lucienne Day, who early in her career sold designs for fashion fabrics, is known to have sold a design to Horrockses, although it is unclear if it was ever produced. A name that appeared several times in the company's business records in the late 1940s is Brooke Cadwallader, a New York-based designer best known for his hand-printed scarves, dress fabrics, accessories and men's ties. He supplied designs to Horrockses Fashions for both cotton and jersey fabrics.

A fabric design added 2d. to the cost of producing a yard of fabric.[44] Evidence from Horrockses Fashions' business records suggests the company bought many designs that never made it to the printers and this was a bone of contention among the board members, ever keen to ensure the company was profitable. Managing director Herbert Mallott complained that 100 designs purchased in 1949 had not been used (this represented half of its annual purchases). James Cleveland Belle and Kurt Lowit's defence of this practice was that they were aiming for originality and novelty and having a large stock of designs, spanning a whole range of styles, was crucial for maintaining the company's competitive edge.[45]

Finishing

Kurt Lowit (2.55) was central to Horrockses Fashions' success. According to Bernard Leser (managing director of Horrockses Fashions (Canada), 1952–6), Lowit was a genius and the company owed him 'a great deal for the high standard of quality we achieved'.[46] Stephanie Godfrey has commented that he was continually experimenting with new weaves, finishes, colours and dyes. He was particularly interested in colour and had an uncanny knack of always being able to predict the correct shades for the next season. It was Lowit's job to liaise with the numerous firms contracted by Horrockses to print its fabrics.[47] During the 1940s and '50s, the company used a variety of printers in the north-west of England, including Bleakleys for quality printing, Bollingtons for quantity, Calico Printers Association mainly for rayon and silk printing, and a variety of others including Hollingsworth, Mark Fletcher and, in the late 1950s, David Whitehead. Jersey

2.56 *A cocktail dress in Sekers'*
nylon from the late 1950s. The
design has been transfer printed.
Courtesy of the Harris Museum
and Art Gallery, Preston:
PRSMG: 2001.35w

fabric was usually printed at Barracks and when transfer printing was introduced in the second half of the 1950s this was completed by Star Stampa Tessuti, Italy (2.56).

It was common for 70 to 80 fabric designs to be used for a collection of 150 to 160 dress styles. The majority of these designs were printed in quantities of 7,000 to 10,000 yards, sometimes with repeat orders placed at a later date.[48] However, it is clear that it was not always easy to get cloth quantities right, as frequently Horrockses seemed to be left with surplus cloth and was often struggling to dispose of it. The finished cloth was required at the making-up factories six weeks prior to the showing of a collection.[49] Machine printing with engraved rollers was the usual method adopted for quantities of 7,200 yards, the larger quantity reflecting the set up costs of engraving rollers; hand-screen printing was reserved for shorter runs of 300 yards per design.[50] Where

colour was of the greatest importance, screen printing was considered to be the best process as it was regarded as being more suitable for fine lines, and it was the favoured technique for the printing of poplins. The fashion designers in London were expected to take into account the cost of fabric per yard and, therefore, to style more expensive cloths simply, 'thus enabling the garment production costs to be reduced and permit the finished garment to remain within the price range of 54/- and 45/- [54 and 45 shillings].'[51]

The strategic use of fabric design in a collection was considered a key means of limiting the quantities of a particular style, helping to disguise the scale of production. This would help to counter a criticism of ready-to-wear, that women would hate to be seen in identical dresses. So the usual practice was to aim to style each fabric 'twice in quite different types of garments' (2.57, 2.58).[52] The fashion

Ivy Mill No. 123.

London Ref No 532.

1½" Belt.

Buttons V1440/24 Black.

14. 16. 18

Cloth No. 16118
16196

gone to factory   belt 1½" wide

Ivy Mill No. 124

London Ref. No. 586

Belt $\frac{3}{4}$"

zip 16"

Belt $\frac{3}{4}$" wide

Cloth No. 1618 1619

Lovely housecoats—lovely cottons, cottons that have an invisible secret magic—thanks to *fine finishing by the B.D.A.* For finishes are the wizardry of today, transforming well-known fibres with new guises: and cotton, as you see it here, is a poor relation no longer.

The B.D.A. are specialists in finishing cottons of every kind. Two of their finishes are already famous—"Quintafix"-crease-shedding, stain-resist, and "Rigmel"-shrunk: but also, keeping pace with the very latest developments, they can give cottons easy-care properties with minimum-iron finishes.

Whatever kind of fabrics you buy, specify "Finished by the B.D.A."—the B.D.A. have finishes for every kind of fibre, both natural and man-made, including acrylics (with the sole exception of silk)—and you'll find the assurance of quality a B.D.A. finish gives is a thoroughly worthwhile investment.

HOUSECOATS BY **Horrockses**

Look for the B.D.A. Red Seal – for the finest in finishing

Previous page
2.57 & 2.58 Horrockses Fashions'
usual practice was to style each
fabric twice in quite different
garments, as can been seen in these
two examples (styles 532 and 536).
Daphne Razzell (née Patten)

2.59 An advertisement for Bradford
Dyers' Association 'Quintafix'
treatment developed in 1952
for Horrockses Fashions.
The Ambassador, no.7, 1957

2.60 Horrockses Fashions' staff
on a day out in Sussex. They are
all wearing Horrockses' dresses.
The woman third from the right
is wearing a dress in a fabric by
Pat Albeck; the one on the far right
wears a dress in a fabric designed
by Joyce Badrocke, 1953–4.
Stephanie Houlgrave

designers were expected to consider the relationship between fashion and fabric designs so '...when a design was being chosen, in addition to considering the spacing of the design careful thought must be given to the ultimate effect when cutting the garment, in order to avoid wastages.'[53]

Kurt Lowit's standards were exacting. New fabrics were always rigorously tested for tensile strength, light and colour fastness, and shrinkage. He was a stickler for correct colour matching by the printers, and faulty orders were required to be reprinted. Lowit was also responsible for the finishes that were applied to the fabrics. It was crucial that its principal cloth – cotton – was easy to look after, particularly in light of creeping competition from emerging fabrics such as nylon. The 1940s and '50s saw a huge number of finishes that were aiming to minimize the labour of looking after ready-made garments. There were crease-resistant finishes, permanent pleating, surface finishes and stiffening, as well as treatments that eliminated shrinkage and improved washability. For cotton, crease resistance was vital to a successful ready-made product and was instrumental in its rising status. A number of treatments were available, including 'Caplreta Crease-Resist' and 'Tebilized'. These were heavily promoted, with swing tags attached to garments detailing the treatment that the fabric had undergone. Surface glazing processes (for example, 'Everglaze') were adopted from furnishings in

the 1940s and applied to cottons and linens to aid crease resistance. These had the added bonus of stiffening the fabric, which was particularly appropriate for the voluminous skirts popular from 1947 onwards. Horrockses Fashions used finishes such as Caplreta from the start. But, by 1951, Lowit was seeking out a better and less stiff finish for Horrockses' cottons. He approached Bradford Dyers' Association (BDA) to develop a finish for a collection of outfits that Horrockses was designing for the Duchess of Kent's tour of the Far East in 1952. Lowit wanted a finish that would allow the clothes to look good straight from the suitcase, and would be able to be laundered easily and not require ironing. The finish was developed by BDA's Joe David and was called 'Quintafix' (2.59). It proved to be very profitable for BDA and successful for Horrockses Fashions.[54]

Horrockses Fashions' success lay in the combination of innovative fabric design, the use of the best quality cotton cloth and the collaboration between fashion and textile designers. The company was steered by the dynamism of James Cleveland Belle, with his ability to spot design talent, and the expertise of Kurt Lowit. The clever use of progressive fabric designs helped to conceal the true mass-produced nature of Horrockses Fashions' output. It enabled the company to fulfil Horrockses, Crewdson & Co.'s objective of using fine cloth to elevate the status of cotton and promote its cotton piece goods (2.60).

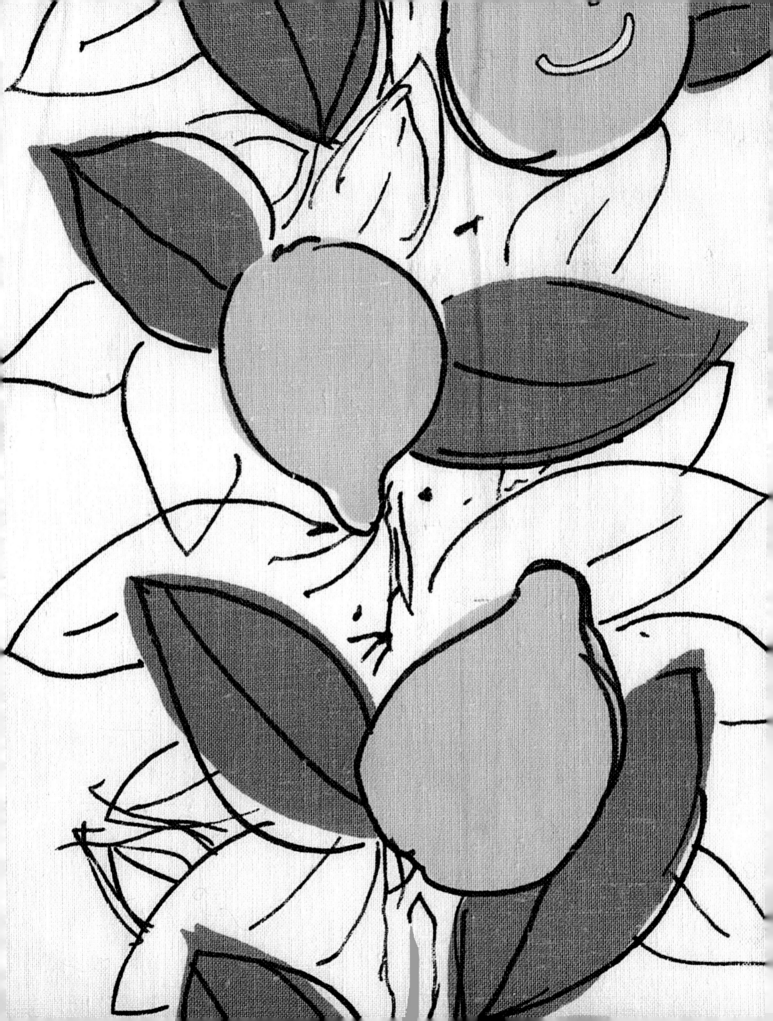

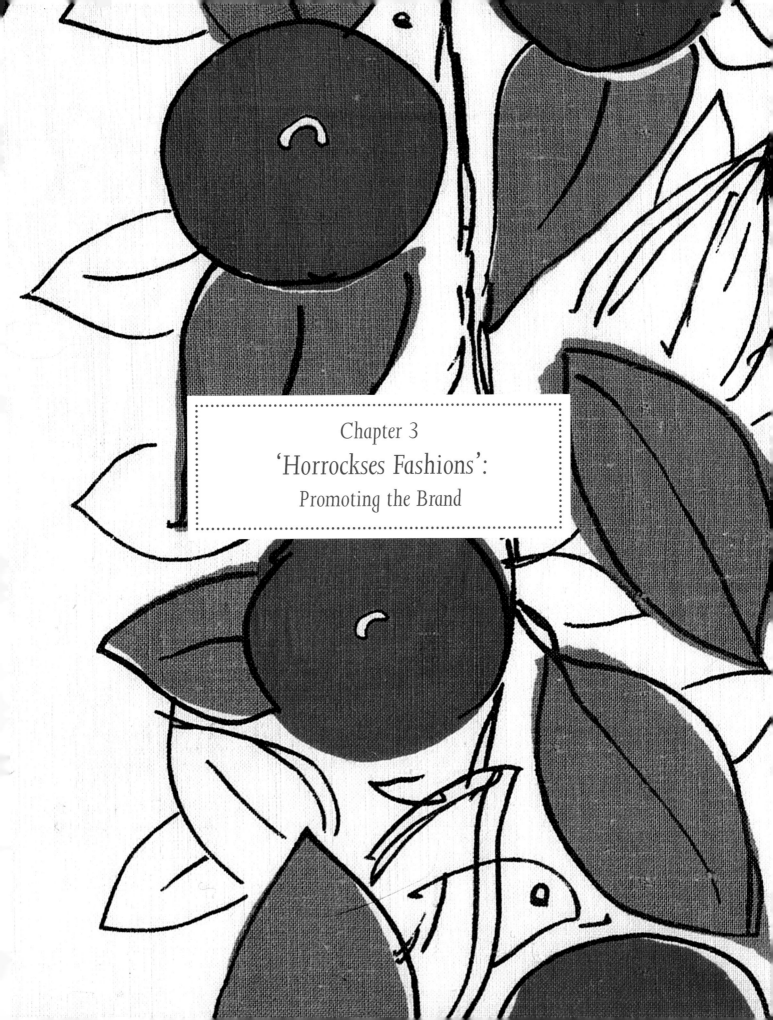

Chapter 3
'Horrockses Fashions':
Promoting the Brand

3.1 *Horrockses had experienced the benefits of associating its products with film stars in the 1930s. Here we see Merle Oberon modelling a dress made from Horrockses 'Nucolaine'.*
Film Fashionland, *August 1934*

The rise of the brand

Margaret Wray reported that, in 1939, 289 firms were producing branded women's wear lines, and these tended to be garments of particularly high quality and price. After the Second World War, the practice became much more widespread and, by 1952, the number of women's wear brands had increased substantially to 866, an increase of over 33 per cent.[1] She has argued that this increase, along with the accompanying rise in advertising, was the most significant development in the clothing industry in the immediate post-war years.[2] Horrockses Fashions was at the centre of these changes and Chapters 3 and 4 explore the ways in which information about the products of a ready-to-wear fashion manufacturer was conveyed to customers, by examining Horrockses' strategies around branding, promotion and retail (3.2). The company endeavoured to convey the message that its garments were a quality product, following couture styling, using exciting fabric designs and all at affordable prices. These values were communicated through carefully considered promotion, incorporating advertising, the production of 'specials' for high-profile customers and the careful choice of retail outlets for the sale of its merchandise.

'Horrockses Fashions':

Promoting the Brand

A Horrockses, Crewdson & Co. director's report of 1944 set out the company's intentions in relation to the development of branded merchandise, '…there is no doubt in the minds of the Board that the future of the Company lies in high-class specialities and branded lines produced by the most efficient and modern methods'.[3] The idea of branding and the promotion of cloth permeated right through the Horrockses, Crewdson & Co. organization, and the importance of 'Horrockses as being available in every phase of cotton – Horrockses' cottons, Horrockses' taffetas, Horrockses' corduroys etc.' was noted.[4] A reputation for quality had been built up by the company throughout the nineteenth century, with drapers' advertising unusually singling out the company by name and frequently citing the term 'quality' in reference to its piece goods: 'Horrockses shirtings and long cloths' or 'Horrockses' calicoes'. Clothing companies noted the use of Horrockses' fabrics in their advertising, for example, J.G. Lamming mentioned 'Super "Contego" Shirts Made to order from Horrockses, Miller & Co.'s Long Cloths.'[5] Horrockses also advertised its own cloths and, by the twentieth century, it was promoting its finished goods, such as sheets and towels, accompanied by the tag line, *The Greatest Name in Cotton*'. Its fashion fabrics

3.2 *A Horrockses Fashions' label.*
Christine Boydell

were advertised extensively with the word 'Horrockses' displayed prominently (3.1). So, by 1946, the name would have been very familiar and it was on this existing reputation for quality that the brand 'Horrockses Fashions' was built. This familiarity meant that customers had certain expectations of a product carrying the name 'Horrockses'.

The notion of branding merchandise was not new. The Trade Marks Registration Act was passed in 1875 and, as well as providing legal protection to the manufacturer, it instilled in goods an element of guarantee as regards quality and helped to differentiate similar products. Branding a product held certain benefits for manufacturers: it allowed them to 'speak' directly to their customers, minimizing the intervention of distributors and consequently helping them to avoid the stranglehold of the wholesaler; it aided the development of customer loyalty, ensuring a steady demand for their product; and it allowed investment and production planning to take place with increased confidence. The aim of branding was to persuade customers to approach retailers with direct requests for particular branded lines. This was achieved by promoting the product widely. In order to ensure customer loyalty, it was essential for the manufacturer to maintain the quality of the product otherwise the label could become a liability rather than an asset. From a customer's point of view, branding allowed them to shop with knowledge in a world where increasing choice was available; once they had purchased a branded item, the expectation was that they would know what to expect from future purchases and remain loyal to that brand. At the beginning of its life, a brand has to rely on its functional qualities and possibly on the reputation of related company brands, as was the case with Horrockses. But, over time, the product should accumulate added value beyond its functional purpose. This added value includes the qualities attributed to the brand through advertising and other promotional activity, and those that are accrued through the experience of use by customers.

The rise of the manufacturer

Before the Second World War, the dominant players in the clothing industry were the distributor (the department store, multiple and variety chains, the small independent retailer and the mail-order firm) and the wholesaler. The wholesaler acted as a middleman, organizing and financing production and supplying the distributor. Due to over-production and fierce competition among manufacturers, the distributors could pick and choose merchandise and became dominant, fixing prices and dictating conditions of supply. The manufacturer tended to be an anonymous player and often it was the retailer's or wholesaler's name that appeared in the garment. However, the war resulted in a change in emphasis in the industry. Shortages, designation and strong wartime demand resulted in a shift in the balance of power in favour of the manufacturer. This was accompanied by a growth in branded merchandise. Manufacturers were keen to increase customer awareness of their products so that they would ask for a specific brand rather than relying on a retailer's choices of stock. Increasingly, they took over the role of wholesalers, selling directly to distributors; consequently, wholesalers virtually disappeared from the industry. This can be illustrated by the experience of Eric Newby's family wholesale business, which by the end of the 1940s was really struggling and finally closed in 1953:

> Now, on every side, new, livelier firms were springing up
> whose principles appreciated the importance of
> promoting their products by giving them brand names
> that were redolent of candle-light and high-living for
> which we were no match. Most of our customers
> removed our labels at any rate, substituting their own.[6]

Horrockses Fashions exemplified this trend towards branded merchandise: designing and manufacturing its own labelled products, utilizing extensive advertising and selling direct to large numbers of retailers in Britain and overseas.

Debates about branding

Great claims were made for branded women's wear in the 1950s, for example, some felt that a branded garment was half sold even before it entered a shop and evidence supplied to the retail trade journal *Fashions and Fabrics* in 1952 suggested that, without branding, a garment stood no chance, 'Retailers say that when style, quality and price are equal, the branded article always sells in preference to the unbranded'. But they went on to note that 'Where the price is lower, however, the unbranded article will be sold easily'.[7] When *Fashions and Fabrics* surveyed its readers on their attitudes to branded merchandise, they reported that three-quarters of the public asked their retailer for particular branded women's wear.[8] So important was satisfying customers' requests that some stores adopted an American technique of inviting customers to leave comments if they could not find the brand they were looking for; the department store chain Owen Owen instigated a scheme whereby customers could complete a leaflet titled 'You didn't have it'.[9]

Stocking branded merchandise held some advantages for the retailer. With unbranded products, the guarantee of quality and fashionable style lay with the retailer in his or her choice of stock, but the presence of the maker's mark on a garment transferred the responsibility for quality to the manufacturer. Now if customers had complaints the problem was referred back to the manufacturer, who was forced to deal with them or face losing an account and threatening its good name. Branded stock was usually accompanied by strong advertising campaigns, with retailers receiving promotional material - anything from

swing tags (which were seen increasingly in the early 1950s), to photographs, brochures, display boards and window display material for special promotions. These activities helped to ensure a high rate of turnover of stock making branded merchandise very attractive to the shop owner.

In spite of such benefits, there was a great deal of suspicion in the retail trade regarding the rise in branded women's wear. While most agreed that branding was useless without adequate promotional campaigns to familiarize the customer with the product, there was some hostility to widespread advertising. In 1953, *Fashions and Fabrics* recorded the view of one shop owner, 'In my opinion branded merchandise is becoming a fetish. Better value, quality and make is obtainable from unbranded sources, but persistent advertising has made the public "brand conscious", and they have fallen for the propaganda that suggests that it must be good if it bears a name'. The shop owner concluded, pessimistically, that 'nothing can stop this trend'.[10] Many felt that the money that went into advertising would be better spent on improving quality and reducing the price of a garment. There were further complaints that manufacturers were negligent in informing retailers of when particular garments were going to be advertised, or that deliveries of orders failed to coincide with advertising campaigns. In addition, retailers criticized manufacturers for their inability to provide sufficiently large orders to support some advertised goods – this reflected manufacturers' practice of overselling and trying out lines before committing their factories to a large production run. There was general agreement from both manufacturer and retailer that quality, and the maintenance of it, was key to the success of a brand. However, there was frequent discontent with the quality of clothes. Some retailers reported that the orders they received were of poorer quality than the sample they had been shown on which their order was based and

3.3 *Horrockses Fashions often supplied*
retailers with display cards such as this
one, which helped support the brand.
Courtesy of the Harris Museum
and Art Gallery, Preston:
PRSMG: 2003.53.3
Photograph by Norwyn Ltd

there was some concern that successful styles were repeated year after year.[11]

During the 1950s, it was claimed by those with a special interest that the altruistic motive behind branding was that it brought down costs and made fashionable clothes more widely available. One such organization was the Branded Merchandise Group (that included Horrockses, Crewdson & Co. as a member), founded in 1946 to protect the interests of manufacturers of branded clothing and textiles. Unsurprisingly, the Group maintained that branded merchandise was 'wholly beneficial'.[12]

Advertising

In order for the customer to recognize a brand, it was crucial that they should have heard about it prior to a shopping trip and advertising was the main method that was used. In 1946, *The Drapers' Record* encouraged readers (manufacturers and retailers) to take the lead from American firms who were advertising widely, with the result that customers were asking for their goods directly.[13] They also published a series of articles on branding in the mid-1940s. With numerous similar products on the market, it was the perceived differences and the added value that a purchaser could acquire as communicated through advertising that were seen as the keys to success. For Horrockses Fashions, the added value consisted of ideas around fabric quality, exclusivity and style. These concepts were imbued in the garments from their conception, in terms of choice of fabrics, fabric pattern and colour, through to their manufacture using the semi-mass production method of making-through (see Chapters 1 and 2). But they were particularly conveyed in the advertising and promotion that followed. Manufacturers such as Horrockses organized their advertising well in advance and provided trade buyers with information on planned promotions, along with display material for their stores (3.3).

This was intended to encourage them to place orders at the beginning of the production season and so minimize the risk of unsold stock. However, not all branded goods were advertised and some manufacturers targeted distributors only, through the trade press, relying on them to promote the brand in their retail outlets and in consumer advertising.

In order to maintain the success of a brand, there were a number of factors that manufacturers needed to address. Firstly, complex forward production planning was required to ensure that stock was available to the customer in retail outlets to coincide with editorial coverage in the press and advertising in magazines; secondly, space needed to be booked in appropriate publications; and thirdly, timely provision of display materials to retailers was required. The pay-off was, hopefully, a larger volume of sales. In addition, a manufacturer who advertised was less likely to have unsold merchandise at the end of the season, as retailers were more willing to stock products that had been heavily advertised. It would appear that advertising was also used to reduce the risks associated with selling clothing where fashionable styling played a dominant role. According to Wray, the typical product of a national advertiser like Horrockses was 'a well-styled garment which has considerable fashion appeal but is eminently wearable…'.[14]

From the outset, Horrockses Fashions promoted its brand through widespread advertising in both the trade press and in women's general interest and fashion magazines. Manufacturers such as Horrockses Fashions were very seasonal in the timing of their advertising, concentrating on September to October for the Autumn/Winter collections and February to March and May for Spring/Summer. Advertisements appeared regularly in the trade press, including *The Ambassador*,[15] *Fashions and Fabrics Overseas*,[16] the *Vogue Book of British Exports* and *The Maker-Up*, while consumer

Horrockses Fashions
REGD.
in Fine Cotton

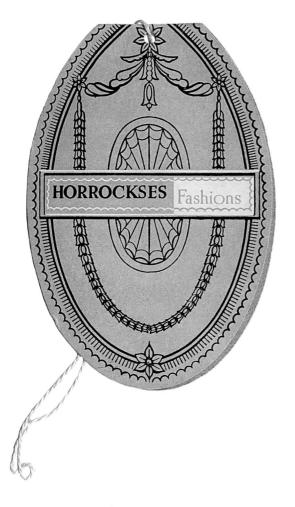

3.4 *An advertisement for Horrockses Fashions.*
Vogue, June 1951

3.5 *This Horrockses Fashions' swing tag was attached to its products in the mid-1950s.*
Courtesy of the Harris Museum and Art Gallery, Preston:
PRSMG: 1997.114
Photograph by Norwyn Ltd

3.6 *This advertisement focuses on the dress and appeared in a 1955 Royal Opera House catalogue, indicating the kind of customer that Horrockses was targeting.*
Royal Opera House

advertising could be found in up-market publications such as *Vogue*, *The Queen*, *Vanity Fair*, *Harper's Bazaar*, *Woman's Journal* and *The Lady*. All of Horrockses' advertising in the 1940s and '50s contained limited text, usually just the words 'Horrockses Fashions', in a simple geometric serifed font. The words 'in Fine Cotton' were usually presented beneath, in a handwritten style harking back to the parent company's long tradition in the cotton business (3.4). This combination communicated the dual messages of traditional values and the modernity of a mass-produced brand. Tradition was also suggested in the design of its swing tags, whose Regency style linked the product to the company's elegant Hanover Square headquarters (3.5). The majority of advertisements included well-known models wearing cotton dresses against plain backgrounds, with the emphasis on the dress (3.6). Sometimes, a prop was added;

3.7 *A 1951 advertisement for a*
Horrockses' cotton dress.
The Ambassador, no.5, 1951

3.8 *A Horrockses Fashions'*
advertisement for a
wool jersey outfit.
Vogue, August 1955
Photograph by Norwyn Ltd

3.9 *A summer dress.*
The Ambassador, no.10, 1951

frequently this was a piece of contemporary furniture (3.7), or occasionally something more traditional. These somewhat contradictory ideas may suggest that the company was not always completely clear about the message it wanted to convey about the Horrockses Fashions' brand. Models were also photographed in exotic locations emphasizing the role of the Horrockses' dress in the summer holiday wardrobe (3.9). Town clothes, particularly for the Autumn/Winter season, were often shot in bustling city streets. As these fashions were frequently made of wool or corduroy, 'Fine cotton' was dropped from the advertisements in favour of 'in Fine Corduroy' or 'in Wool Jersey' (3.8).

3.10 The model 'Raffles' wears a
Horrockses' cotton shirtwaister in
this publicity photograph.
Zoltan Glass

3.11 Barbara Goalen, one of the most well known fashion models of the
1950s, advertises a Horrockses Fashions' evening dress.
Vogue, October 1952

It was no accident that the styles adopted in Horrockses Fashions' advertising demonstrated strong parallels with the photography used to illustrate couture fashions in prestige fashion magazines such as *Vogue* and *Harper's Bazaar*. Such associations could also be seen in the choice of models employed for both advertising and publicity shots. Barbara Goalen, possibly the most iconic model of the period, appeared in several Horrockses Fashions' advertisements (3.11). Other models included Sarah Abraham, Jean Dawnay, Pat Goddard, Ann Gunning, Jennifer Howland, 'Raffles' and Sheelagh Wilson.

In her book, *Model Girl*, Dawnay describes her audition in 1947 for the company: 'Miss Edwards [*sic*] produced one of the prettiest dresses I had ever seen, let alone worn, and asked me [to] try it on… I felt like Cinderella in this cotton frock'. She was asked to model it for some visiting buyers and was then offered a job working three days a week for 4½ guineas.[17] Early Horrockses Fashions' photography was undertaken by Zoltan Glass (3.10), as well as by the George Miles Studio, David Olins and H.R. Clayton Limited. But, most frequently, the company employed the services of John French, whose characteristic

Horrockses Fashions
from our Autumn Collection

3.12 *A full-skirted dress with an abstract print, Spring 1956.* Photograph by John French.
AAD/1995/16/3/4

3.13 This photograph of *Ann Gunning modelling a Horrockses' summer dress shows John French's 'improvements'.*
John French. *AAD/9/79/3703-6B*

Overleaf (left)
3.14 Occasionally, *Horrockses Fashions used illustrations in advertisements to capture the romanticism of its creations. This one was drawn by the Daily Express illustrator, 'Robb'.*
Vogue, June 1949

Overleaf (right)
3.15 *An illustration by 'Robb'.*
The Queen, 2 March 1949

cleanliness and purity of lighting perfectly suited Horrockses' clean and crisp cotton creations (3.12). French's perfectionism was legendary and all of his photographs were 'improved' by extensive re-touching (3.13). Sometimes Horrockses adopted illustration-style advertising, with artwork by the well-known *Daily Express* newspaper illustrator, 'Robb'. These were romantic in tone and emphasized voluminous swinging skirts (3.14, 3.15).

Advertising was an additional cost but was considered vital in order to get a brand known and to keep it in the public eye. Figures compiled by Wray indicate that the majority of firms (47 per cent) spent over £2,000 per year on advertising, while 30 per cent spent over £5,000.[18] Although precise details of

Horrockses Fashions
REGD.

in Fine Cotton

Horrockses Fashions

REGD.

in Fine Cotton

Children's Wear
by
Pirouette PRODUCTIONS LTD.

A **Horrockses** SUBSIDIARY

Nylon . . .

the universal choice for

lingerie and blouses . . .

now created

as luxury dress fabrics

for all occasions . . .

new 'fluid' Nylons

by

Dress in "Chevronyl" by Horrockses Fashions Ltd.

Pampalon . . . Crocolon

. . . Cotillon . . .

Barrelon . . . Chevronyl

Fluonyl . . . Crepnyl

WEST CUMBERLAND SILK MILLS LIMITED · WHITEHAVEN · ENGLAND
LONDON SHOWROOMS: 29 BRUTON STREET, W.1
MAYFAIR 6744/5/6

THE AMBASSADOR

OH, YES! AND IT RESISTS SHRINKAGE AND SHEDS CREASES, TOO

Certainly, cotton sells on fashion appeal and looks. But cotton sells even better when it has that extra something that modern science can give it —the amiable ability to shed creases. That's the wonderful advantage of "Quintafix"-finish by the B.D.A. With this invisible magic, cottons shed creases, resist shrinkage, keep clean longer. What a selling PLUS! Don't miss out on this one—make sure that *your* cottons are "Quintafix"-finished.

Make sure, too, that everybody knows the crease-shedding virtues of the cottons you sell—explain all round that because they're "Quintafix"-finished they shed creases, resist shrinkage, keep clean longer.

DRESS & JACKET BY

Horrockses
•
"Quintafix"
crease-shedding
finish by the
B.D.A.

THE BRADFORD DYERS'
ASSOCIATION, LIMITED, ENGLAND

THE AMBASSADOR

3.16 *An advertisement for Horrockses Pirouette.*
Vogue, June 1951

3.17 *An example of Horrockses Fashions benefiting from advertising by the fabric supplier, Sekers.*
The Ambassador, no.9, 1952

3.18 *Bradford Dyers' Association was commissioned to develop a crease-shedding finish by Horrockses Fashions. The result was 'Quintafix', advertised here using a Horrockses' outfit designed by John Tullis's assistant, Gloria Smythe.*
The Ambassador, no.3, 1955

Horrockses Fashions' outlay on advertising have not survived, expenditure on advertising was mentioned in the company's management meeting minutes on more than one occasion; in 1951, Herbert Mallott, commented 'that a very high proportion of our costs were in Advertising and publicity'.[19] Also in 1951, the firm estimated that it cost approximately 2 shillings per garment to advertise a dress that cost on average £3 to produce. To put this into the context of other costs involved, the fabric for the average summer dress was 30 shillings, while the average profit on each garment was 14 shillings.[20] We do know that the parent company's other subsidiary, R.H. Reynolds Brothers Limited, was expecting to spend about £3,000 on advertising in 1950, on its cheaper product. At that time, a colour full-page advertisement in *The Drapers' Record* cost £51, while *Fashions and Fabrics* charged £33.10s.[21] In 1950, Horrockses Fashions spent £1,800 on advertising its children's wear, recently branded as 'Horrockses Pirouette' (3.16).[22] It seems likely, therefore, that for its main product, women's wear, the company would have spent considerably more. Occasionally, Horrockses Fashions worked cooperatively with other firms and consequently received additional exposure in their advertising. Horrockses' dresses in non-cotton fabrics were included in Sekers' advertisements (3.17), and Bradford Dyers' Association, who had initially developed the 'Quintafix' finish for Horrockses, frequently illustrated Horrockses Fashions' products in their promotions (3.18).

3.19 *An invitation (designed by Joyce Badrocke) to Horrockses Fashions' 1952 showing of its summer collection.*
AAD/2009/4

3.20 *A fashion show at 15 St George Street, Hanover Square, with Segnion modelling a jersey evening gown, c.1947.*
Central Press Photos Ltd

Horrockses Fashions Limited
will present their
Summer 1952 Collection
Town and Country Dresses, Housecoats, Beachwear, Separates
Daily from Thursday, 6th March, 1952
at 10.30 a.m. and 2.30 p.m.
15 St. George Street, Hanover Square, W.1

R.S.V.P. Printed Card Enclosed   *Mayfair 7535*

Journalism

Editorial in magazines and newspapers brought branded women's wear to the customers' attention and Horrockses Fashions was regularly included in the fashion pages of the daily press as well as in specialist fashion magazines. Magazine journalists and newspaper editors played an important intermediary role in providing customers with information and advice about fashion: they influenced what became fashionable and provided vital publicity for manufacturers of ready-to-wear. For branded merchandise, it was critical that customers

were not only aware of the existence of a brand, but that they also knew where they could purchase it. Therefore, magazines and newspapers would provide this information, often including the price of the garment. For example, *The Daily Sketch* included a section on their fashion page called 'Where to get them', and in their coverage of Horrockses Fashions' first collection, *The Tatler* informed its readers that 'Lillywhites will have this dress in stock later this month'.[23]

A manufacturer needed to foster good relationships with the press and, to this end, Horrockses provided 'specials' for

several fashion journalists, including Iris Ashley of the *Daily Mail*, Pat Creed and Audrey Withers of *Vogue* and Elsbeth Juda of *The Ambassador*.[24] Fashion shows were held exclusively for the press, who were supplied with photographs, illustrations (often drawn by Daphne Patten) and information on when and where the clothes could be purchased in the hope that fashion editors would publish information on Horrockses' latest collection (3.19). The fashion show was an extremely important promotional tool for a fashion company. Horrockses usually held its shows at its London headquarters (3.20). During the 1940s, it organized one for retail buyers and one for the press, with invitations also being offered to women in the public eye. In 1951, it was decided to divide the press shows into two: one for the magazines and one for the newspapers, highlighting the significance of these intermediaries to a fashion business. Occasionally, a show would include two or three designs that were not put into production but were purely for prestige purposes. These garments tended to be a little more complex in terms of construction and not cost effective for mass production.

Promotional activity in the newspapers included competitions that featured Horrockses Fashions. *Empire News* held several in 1952, readers were invited to arrange a number of dresses in order of merit. The winning entries had to match the order chosen by the paper's fashion editor, Lillian Hill. Cash prizes could be won, as well as consumer goods such as TV sets, refrigerators and holidays. The dresses and swimsuits were 'modelled' by stars of the Rank organization, including Petula Clark, Barbara Murray and Joan Collins.[25]

Specials

Horrockses Fashions regarded the production of 'specials' for customers as a key method of gaining publicity for its brand. The company provided individually fitted examples from its main collection, or occasionally a bespoke design (3.21). James Cleveland Belle's and John Tullis's contacts in the world of entertainment were crucial and a surviving measurement book demonstrates the scale of this side of the company's business: 93 names are listed with measurements and contact details; women from the world of theatre and film are included, such as Coral Brown, Dora Bryan, Gladys Cooper, Ann Crawford, Margot Fonteyn, Joan Greenwood and Vivien Leigh, along with those from the aristocracy.[26] Under the direction of John Tullis, dresses were created for several West End shows, for example, *The Millionairess* staring Katharine Hepburn in 1952. But the production of specials needed to be balanced against the publicity they were able to generate. The two or three fittings required and the making-up took the valuable time of Hanover Square staff, with regular complaints that the production of specials interfered with the main business of the company, volume production.

Promotional tie-ins

The notion of exploiting the commercial possibilities of film was imported from Hollywood, where by the late 1930s it was possible to purchase mass-produced versions of styles worn by stars in many films through retail outlets such as Bernard Waldman's Modern Merchandising Bureau and Cinema Fashions Stores. In Britain in the 1930s, magazines such as *Film Fashionland* and *Women's Filmfair* provided customers with advice on how to copy film-star looks and ready-made versions of cinema fashions and dressmaking patterns via mail-order. The value of promotional tie-ins with film was becoming increasingly popular in the late 1940s in Britain. In April 1947, *The Drapers' Record* illustrated the 'Phillipa' hat designed by Hugh Beresford and worn by the actress Greta Gynt in the Rank production *Take My Life*, noting that 'the hat will be available to retailers'.[27] According to author Margaret Disher, the first genuine fashion tie-in with a British film appeared in the intriguingly titled 1948 Rank feature, *Warnings to Wantons*.[28] A negligee worn by the French star Anne Vernon was sponsored by Slenderella, who produced a number of

PICTURE POST

RONA ANDERSON:
A STAR
FROM
SCOTLAND

4 WEEK ENDING
12 MARCH 1955

HOW TO CUT THE PRICE OF FOOD
BENNY HILL: HITTING THE TV JACKPOT
OUR TWELVE PERSONALITY GIRLS ON PARADE

HULTON'S
NATIONAL
WEEKLY
EVERY
WEDNESDAY

3.22 The front cover of Picture Post. The actress, Rona
Anderson, is wearing a Horrockses Fashions' housecoat.
Picture Post, 17 March 1955

3.23 The actress, Beatrice
Campbell, modelling a Horrockses
Fashions' outfit in a 1948
advertisement.
The Ambassador, no 6, 1948

3.24 Dinah Sheridan in a publicity photograph for the 1951
Royal Performance film, Where No Vultures Fly. She
wore Horrockses Fashions' outfits throughout the film and
the company's name appeared in the credits.
British Film Institute

exact copies for sale throughout the country to coincide with the release of the film. Some retailers produced window displays of the garment supported by large film stills.

Rank had set up a fashion publicity department in the mid-1940s, mainly to promote its stars dressed in clothes designed for particular films. Its exploitation department developed this further by linking with fashion manufacturers who used Rank stars to advertise and promote their products; Joan Collins from the Rank Charm School was featured regularly on the fashion pages of a number of film magazines modelling Horrockses' outfits.[29] The company also had links with ABC Films and one of its stars, Beatrice Campbell, appeared in a 1948 advertisement for Horrockses Fashions (3.23). Horrockses, Crewdson & Co. had used film stars in advertisements in the 1930s and Horrockses Fashions enjoyed a fruitful relationship with the British film industry in the late 1940s and early '50s, its garments appearing in several films. Sometimes the company created an outfit for an individual actress, as in *Madness of the Heart* (1949) for Margaret Lockwood, or it supplied all the women's clothes for a film, as with *It Always Rains on Sunday* (1947) with Googie

Withers, *Penny and the Pownall Case* (1947), and the 1949 crime thriller *Third Time Lucky*. A lucrative cinematic association for Horrockses Fashions was its involvement with the 1951 film, *Where No Vultures Fly*. The company's name appeared in the credits and the film was screened as the Royal Performance film of 1951. The film's location in Kenya saw the Payton family locked in a battle to save local wildlife, while undermined by locals who were encouraged to hunt for profit by an unscrupulous white ivory hunter. The female lead, played by Dinah Sheridan, wears Horrockses Fashions' clothing throughout and a number of stills available to film exhibitors and the local press saw her posed prominently in these designs (3.24). The film's distributors acquired promotional material from Horrockses Fashions that could be included in cinema foyer displays. E.W. McDermott of the Victoria Cinema, Preston put on such a display for two weeks prior to the film opening and, presumably due to the Preston connection, he was able to include some dresses. Mallott noted that 'we certainly got a lot of advertising from it... it is a pity this cannot be done in all the towns *Where No Vultures Fly* is being shown'.[30]

"The Simple Cotton Dress"

Her Majesty The Queen and the Duke of Edinburgh proceed on their journey amongst the peoples of the Commonwealth. Each port of call, each country visited produces news of the Royal Progress.

One of the earliest "fashion flashes" was of the dress The Queen couldn't do without, or so it seemed, for in photograph after photograph she appeared in

Visiting a children's hospital on Bermuda Island.

the simple but elegant cotton dress by Horrockses Fashions Ltd., London, W.1. This dress is one of several from this firm's new collection chosen by The Queen for the tour.

Readers are reminded of our "Extraordinary edition" - 1954 to be published immediately after the return to Britain of the Royal couple. In that issue we hope to publish the background story to the Royal Tour, and we want to show how British merchandise is promoted during the Royal visit in department stores, fashion shops, men's outfitters and even in the small village "general store".

Our readers in countries The Queen is visiting, are asked once more to send us a full story of the promotions they have staged or are arranging, and to let us have relevant pictures and details.

3.25 *A sketch of one of the dresses chosen by Queen Elizabeth II for her tour of the Commonwealth in 1953–4. Insert shows a photograph of the Queen wearing one of Horrockses' dresses in Bermuda in December 1953.*

The Ambassador, no.1, 1954

3.26 *The Duchess of Kent chose 10 Horrockses Fashions' creations for her tour of the Far East in 1952.*

William Parrott, The Pictorial Story of The HRH The Duchess of Kent's Far East Tour with HRH The Duke of Kent: an Eye Witness Account

The Queen's dresses

Publicizing your product worn on the back of a famous film actress was one thing, but getting royalty into your dresses guaranteed extensive coverage in the press. Members of the royal family frequently chose off-the-peg creations from Horrockses. It was Kathleen Molyneux's (the company's directrice) idea to write to the then Princess Elizabeth with the suggestion that she might like to see a collection of cotton dresses for her forthcoming Commonwealth tour of 1952. Cut short by the death of her father King George VI, she continued her tour towards the end of 1953, taking with her several off-the-peg Horrockses Fashions' dresses (3.25), which

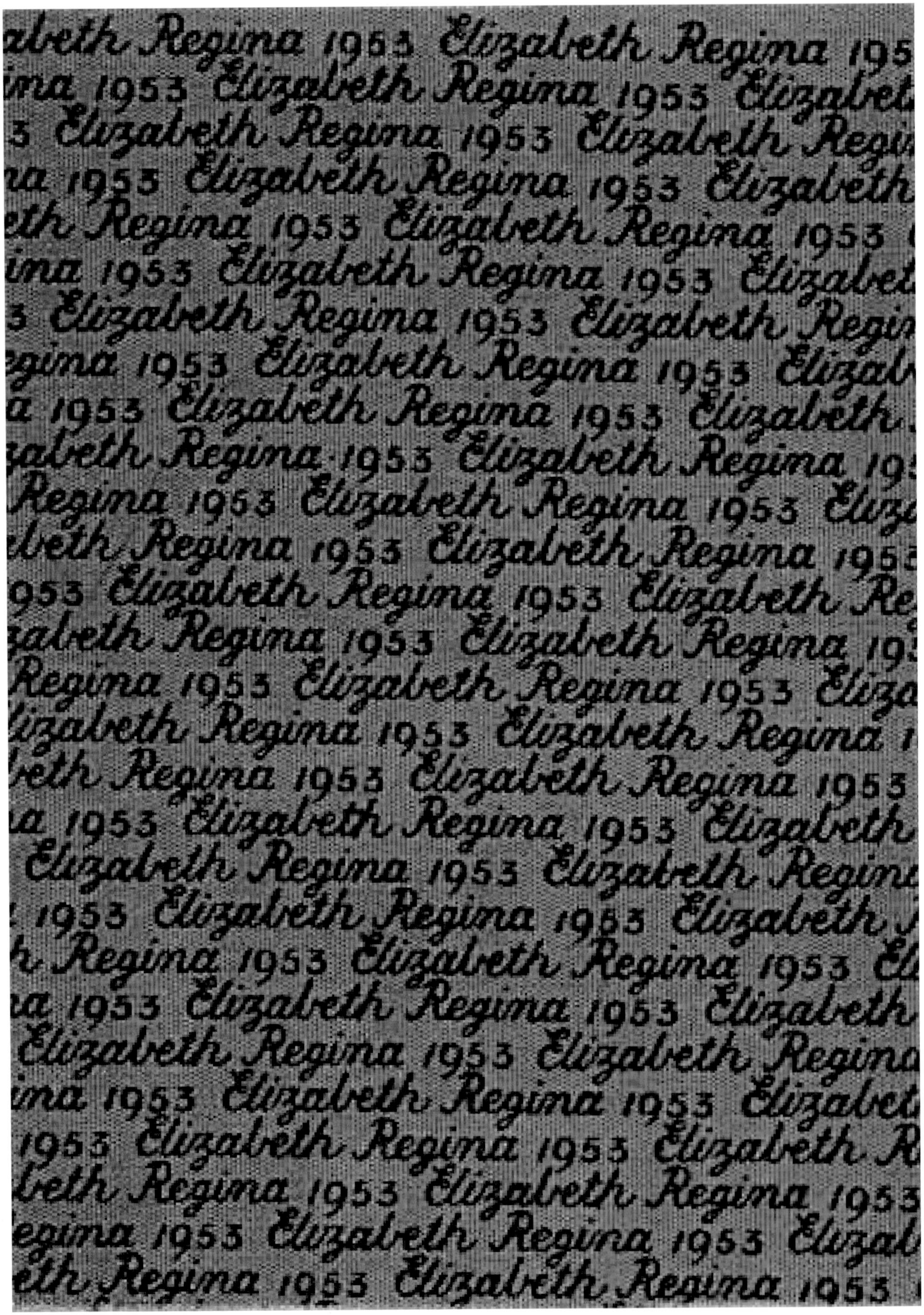
Elizabeth Regina 1953

3.27 This fabric was designed to
commemorate the coronation of
Queen Elizabeth II in 1953.
Jean Grinsted

were subsequently made available to the public at a relatively modest £4.14s.6d. The company's measurement book includes names of other members of the British aristocracy, including Princess Margaret, the Duchess of Gloucester, the Countess of Harewood and the Duchess of Rutland. The Duchess of Kent often wore Horrockses Fashions' dresses and, in 1952, when she undertook a tour of the Far East, she was persuaded to promote British cottons abroad. Along with dresses by Norman Hartnell and John Cavanagh, she chose 10 Horrockses' creations that were illustrated and commented on in the press (3.26). She favoured Horrockses again two years later, as did her daughter, Princess Alexandra, when they visited Canada and America.

Horrockses' dresses were chosen on the condition that similar ones would not be available for sale until they had been worn by the royal family member. In connection with the Queen's 1953–4 Commonwealth tour, the *Daily Mirror* reported that store buyers had been informed that the Queen would be wearing Horrockses' dresses, but they were not told which specific ones had been chosen. Such a strategy encouraged buyers to order a good selection of styles in the hope that 'at least one would be a dress that had taken the Queen's fancy'.[31] In 1954, Horrockses successfully sued the *Daily Sketch* over an article in the paper on 5 December 1953, which claimed that Horrockses had allowed examples of dresses chosen by the Queen for this tour to be sold in the West End of London before she had worn them. It was established that the dress for sale, although from the same collection as the Queen's choices, was not one that she had chosen.[32] Royal associations were developed in a number of fabric designs originated by Horrockses. For coronation year in 1953, the company developed a design using the words 'Elizabeth Regina 1953', which was repeated as continuous stripes across the width of the fabric, printed in black on grounds of rose red, midnight blue or a deep green (3.27). In the same year, another design of daffodils, thistles, shamrocks and roses was produced.

3.28 *A 1956 advertisement for Horrockses Pirouette for teenagers.*
Vogue, March 1956

3.29 *An advertisement for Horrockses Pirouette.*
Vogue, May 1953

Horrockses Pirouette

Following the success of Horrockses Fashions in promoting the parent company's cotton, a related brand was developed with similar values. The parent company had been manufacturing children's cotton clothing through their subsidiary, R.H. Reynolds Brothers, as 'Horrockses Children's Garments'. In 1952, it was decided to associate the higher class children's range more closely with Horrockses Fashions, promoting 'the same fine cut that has become associated with Horrockses Fashions' adult range'.[33] The brand name 'Horrockses Pirouette' was adopted for high quality clothing for children and teenagers (3.28, 3.29). In 1955, Horrockses commissioned members of the Incorporated Society of London Fashion Designers to design the range, with contributions from Giuseppe Mattli, Victor Stiebel, Ronald Patterson and John Cavanagh, signalling clearly the kind of association it wished for the brand.[34] In the same year, *Vogue* introduced Janey Ironside to Horrockses Pirouette and she designed a range that the company produced for the magazine. The collection was described as reflecting 'the simple best of adult fashion, because it abides by these constant criteria of taste: good colours, bright or dark; fine fabrics; simple cut...',[35] and in a feature in the magazine some of the fashions were modelled by Ironside's 11-year-old daughter, Virginia. Ironside went on to design two more collections for Horrockses Pirouette. The links between the two brands were reinforced in 1953, when Horrockses launched some matched styles for mother and daughter, an idea imported from the USA (3.30).

Maintaining brand values

In order to maintain success, a manufacturer of a brand had to ensure that the product always matched customer expectations. Therefore, Horrockses Fashions had to continually reinforce the key values of the brand: quality, easy-care, exclusivity and style. This was particularly important in the face of growing competition from brands such as Sambo, Polly Peck and Linzi. Sustaining quality in all aspects of the Horrockses' product, from fabric and finish to make-up, was vital. From its inception, Horrockses Fashions set store by the fact that its fabrics did not shrink, were colour-fast, easy to launder and treated with a finish to achieve 'Permanent Crispness', and the management meetings make constant references to these qualities. For example, after some debate, Horrockses decided to use 'dry-clean only' labels in its rayon jersey dresses. The concern was that the company was renowned for the easy-care qualities of its better-known cotton lines and was not keen to lose customer confidence.[36]

The make-up of the garments was monitored closely with cut-make-and-trim (CMT) merchandise checked at Ivy Mill before being dispatched to Horrockses' customers. Horrockses Fashions' labels were removed from any dresses that were regarded as sub-standard. So it was a problem when it was discovered that some unscrupulous CMT firms were saving the exclusive Horrockses' fabrics by simplifying patterns and cutting seam allowances. With the surplus fabric they were making cut-price dresses, which were being sold on as 'Horrockses'.[37] Sometimes, damaged cloth was returned to the printers, but they often sold it on and consequently it could be used for sub-standard goods, threatening Horrockses' good name. On one occasion, Horrockses Fashions' fabrics had been spotted on 'dolls at a Pleasure Fair'; such a situation was regarded as unacceptable and it was agreed that 'the closest possible control should be exercised over any cloth printed to our instructions and that material unsuitable for use in our making-up factories should be disposed of in Export markets... protecting Horrockses' name'.[38] On another occasion, it was decided that damaged jersey cloth would be retained and made into scarves to be sold to the company's staff.[39] The disposal of surplus cloth seemed to be a constant problem. One suggestion, to use it for cheap frocks and sold in the sales, was met with short shrift and the comment that it 'would militate against Horrockses Fashions' high class trade'.[40]

Despite the fact that Horrockses Fashions was a mass producer, it went to great lengths to play down the fact. This was evident in its advertising, but it also paid careful attention to details of styling and to producing one style in different fabrics, thereby limiting quantities of each garment. In the *Daily Mail*, in 1953, the paper's fashion editor, Iris Ashley, reported from Madeira that Horrockses Fashions was well represented. She had counted 41 of its designs on tourists and only three were identical![41] It was always a fine balancing act, weighing up the profits to be made from successful volume production against the veneer of exclusivity that it was at pains to promote. The reality of a ready-to-wear operation such as Horrockses Fashions was strict production planning, with careful choice of fabric and styles to disguise the mass production reality. However, it made sure that planning was not 'too rigid or the outstanding qualities of the Horrockses Fashions range might

be jeopardised'.[42] To this end, the company maintained some flexibility in its ranges in order to be able to respond quickly to fashion trends. The fact that it chose carefully the outlets it supplied was also key.

The names of the three Horrockses Fashions' designers rarely appeared in publicity. Even though Horrockses had appointed John Tullis because of his experience in couture, his name and his connections were not promoted. Herbert Mallott wrote to Kathleen Molyneux to complain about a feature in *Vogue*, where a dress was described as 'being designed by John Tullis'. He stipulated that she ensure 'that a Horrockses' fashion production is, in future, described as such and that no reference is made to the individual who created it... I must stress that the goodwill of our Fashion business must remain in the name of Horrockses and not in anyone who is employed by us'.[43]

The brand was everything and communicating clearly its values to potential customers was paramount, particularly in the face of increasing numbers of companies competing in the ready-to-wear market. Horrockses Fashions' decision to promote its product by playing down the reality of its mass manufacture was an appropriate strategy for the selling of women's ready-to-wear, given that most customers were not prepared to be seen wearing identical outfits to other women. The association with glamorous film stars and the social cachet of royal patronage helped to create the impression that by purchasing a Horrockses Fashions' dress a customer was buying something exceptional. This was achieved by a combination of effective promotion and a quality product priced at a level that was affordable for many women. The extent to which the careful distribution of Horrockses Fashions' merchandise supported this message and the success of its communication to customers is examined in Chapter 4.

Chapter 4
'Our Best Dresses':
The Retail and Purchase of Ready-to-Wear

4.2 Dorothy Taylor in a Horrockses
Fashions' sundress (print by
Alastair Morton) on holiday
in Torquay.
Mr John Taylor

Women who chose Horrockses Fashions dresses in the 1940s and '50s speak of them with much fondness. They comment on the quality of the fabrics, the styling, and the vibrant colours and patterns (4.1). Many recall the sense of pleasure in choosing, purchasing, wearing and even ironing these dresses. The overriding impression is that customers felt that the acquisition of a Horrockses' dress was something special, which is why so many women have kept them for over 50 years (4.2). A Horrockses' dress was a sophisticated garment with couture associations, made from high quality fabrics (predominantly cotton), printed with exclusive designs, but available at a reasonable price. There is a clear correspondence between this message and customers' expectations and experience of the brand, as evidenced by the memories of those women who purchased Horrockses Fashions' products.

'Our Best Dresses':
The Retail and Purchase of Ready-to-Wear

Women and femininity in the 1940s and '50s
During the Second World War, many women from all walks of life had taken on jobs vacated by men who had joined the forces, or they themselves had joined up. But in the immediate post-war period, they were encouraged to return to domestic duties. The New Look fashion, featuring dresses with nipped-in waists, huge skirts and soft, sloping shoulders, was a visual representation of this tendancy. However, the look had been anticipated in the late 1930s and early '40s. *Vogue* ran a feature on 'Sloping Shoulders' in 1941,[1] and many designs for evening dresses featured romantically inspired floating skirts that emphasized the waist. The New Look was a natural evolution of these trends, which had been delayed by wartime exigencies. But the style is noteworthy for what it signified about femininity

in the late 1940s and 50s. It was used in advertising and in women's magazines to suggest both glamour *and* domesticity. When worn with voluminous underskirts, corsetry to reduce the waist and high heels, it suggested an exaggerated sexuality. When modelled by women in advertisements for food and household items and in articles about family life, it emphasized a woman's role as homemaker. Sometimes domesticity and glamour were combined, particularly in advertisements for consumer goods, and helped to suggest that household chores were not real work. As the New Look has been so frequently associated with Horrockses Fashions' output, the values attached to it need to be considered when assessing the company's messages about its product and how these messages were adopted, or translated, by the women who bought the clothes.[2] While Horrockses Fashions' advertising emphasized the glamorous and stylish, it also featured the practical and domestic, with frequent mentions of the easy-care qualities and durability of its cotton cloth, which was often printed with floral designs. In this way, the advertisements reflected the contradictory messages presented to women during this period.

The retail of ready-to-wear in the 1940s and '50s
Between Horrockses Fashions and the women who wore its products was the retailer, and advertising was the manufacturer's direct line to the customer. The retail of ready-to-wear fashion brought with it specific problems not faced by other merchandise. Most manufacturers of mass-produced goods relied for success on large-scale production of a limited number of products. Fashion was completely different, primarily

because women were not prepared to be seen wearing identical styles. It was crucial, therefore, that a manufacturer such as Horrockses selected carefully where its products were sold in order to minimize the impact of its volume production. By the middle of the twentieth century, the increasing popularity of ready-to-wear and of branded fashion was beginning to have an impact on the way fashion was retailed.

As the century progressed, improved road transport allowed the more efficient distribution of clothing to retail outlets around the country and enabled customers to travel more easily into town and city centres, encouraging the demand for ready-to-wear. The relationship between manufacturers, wholesalers and distributors of fashionable clothing also changed, impacting on how Horrockses' products reached customers. Developments during the Second World War had seen a decline in the dominance of the wholesaler, resulting in manufacturers such as Horrockses Fashions increasingly dealing directly with retailers. This was accompanied by growing numbers of producers alerting customers to their products by branding and advertising; the hope was that customers would ask retailers for their products when shopping. Margaret Wray illustrated this tendency by quoting a manufacturer who had reported to *Women's Wear News* in 1945 that, with branding, 'Women learn to appreciate a certain make of coat, suit or dress and will remain faithful to it for life…'.[3] At least, that was its aim.

The mid-twentieth century was characterized by four main groups of retailers selling women's and children's clothing. James Jefferys identified these as: department stores, multiple and variety chains, Co-operative shops, and unit retailers (small-scale operations, including independent retailers, sometimes known as 'madam' shops).[4] Horrockses Fashions' products were retailed by all except the Co-operative group. During the inter-war years, distributors, especially the department stores,

had developed a rigid buying system for fashion. Garments were purchased on a seasonal basis: initial orders for Autumn/ Winter were placed in May, for Spring/Summer in October, with half-yearly sales in January and July, and additional small orders placed at various points during the year.

Madam shops

During the 1940s and '50s, there was a definite shift in which companies had the greatest share of the market as far as distributors were concerned. The privately owned dress shop (or madam shop) dominated the retail of women's clothing, mainly because of the desire for individuality in fashion. Jefferys estimated that 'unit retailers' dominated the market with a share of 46 to 55 per cent in 1938, but that this share had been gradually diminishing over the course of a century.[5] Madam shops maintained a personalized approach to selling. This was particularly important in the retail of fashion, where proprietors knew their regular customers extremely well. This meant that they could recommend certain styles, look out for merchandise that would suit individual clients and include a variety of stock that gave the impression that a customer was receiving less standardized products than from the larger retail outlets. Their small-scale orders meant they could respond quickly to customer tastes. But the independent retailers, though still significant, saw a continuing decline in their share of the market after the war in favour of the department store and the multiple shop retailer, who were able to place large advance orders.[6] Smaller concerns complained that even if they did manage to secure an account the manufacturer was reluctant to supply them with specials, small orders or extra garments. However, madam shops preferred the manufacturer-advertised and price-maintained merchandise, as they felt it made their job of selling easier.[7] While small independents managed to compete with the larger chains and

department stores with respect to their low overheads and the personal relationships with their customers, this was set against the disadvantages of not being able to carry a wide range of stock and of often being located away from the main shopping thoroughfare due to high rents.

Multiple chains

From 1930 to 1950, there was a significant increase in the number of multiple chain stores, whose sales of women's and children's wear increased by 118 per cent between 1947 and 1950 and by a further 80 per cent between 1950 and 1954.[8] The multiples had an advantage over the madam shop in that they could place large orders for thousands of identical lines but dilute their impact by distributing them across all their branches. A number of chains were established during the inter-war years, for example, C&A and the Guinea Gown Shops. Morrisons Associated Companies were significant players and retailed in 122 outlets trading under various names, including Graftons, Russells and Kings.[9] Other familiar names included Dorothy Perkins, Etam and Richard Shops, who Jefferys estimates had between 50 and 100 branches each by 1950, sometimes buying up independent madam shops. Many had centralized buying departments, which made for economies of scale that could be passed on to the customer and meant that there was the potential of large orders for manufacturers. According to

Jefferys, these shops were clean and attractive, and maintained high standards of window display and lighting.[10]

Variety chains

Variety chains selling a range of goods, such as Littlewoods, British Home Stores and Marks & Spencer, expanded considerably before the Second World War and became increasingly significant in the retail of ready-to-wear in the immediate post-war period (although Horrockses Fashions never sold to this sector). Marks & Spencer was particularly influential. In 1949, it decided to make fashionable clothing with mass appeal a key activity. The company was highly organized with a cloth buying department that liaised with firms to produce fabric to its own specifications. The print design department was responsible for the selection of designs for dress fabrics, while the design department, established in 1948, originated garment designs and prepared them for mass production, as well as liaising with clothing manufacturers who sometimes originated designs.[11]

Department stores

Department stores were the early pioneers of ready-made clothing (4.3). Jefferys estimated that there were around 500 department stores in the United Kingdom by 1950, with the most significant merchandise in terms of sales being women's

and girl's wear and drapery, representing 40 to 50 per cent of their total turnover and a 20 to 23 per cent share of the market.[12] Originally aiming at the middle-class customer, many had widened their appeal and, by 1950, could be roughly divided between those catering for the 'high-medium' class of trade and those for the 'medium-low' class. In the mid-1920s, a number of amalgamations took place, resulting in a multiple department store arrangement dominated by the Debenhams group, the United Drapery Stores group and Selfridge Provincial Stores (becoming John Lewis Ltd in 1940). The Great Northern and Southern Stores Ltd was established in 1936 and House of Fraser bought up a number of independent retailers in the late 1940s. The Lewis's group also developed a chain of nationwide stores (4.4). Department stores held the advantages of convenience, with a wide range of goods under one roof, and of being centrally located in towns and cities.

Many department stores continued to run making-up departments while buying in from manufacturers such as Horrockses. For example, in 1953, Dickins & Jones still employed 130 dressmakers, tailoresses, milliners, machinists,

corsetieres, lingerie makers and alteration workers suggesting that, in spite of the growth in ready-to-wear fashions, a bespoke service was still desired.[13] But the ability of the department stores to place large orders, often through a centrally organized buying department, meant that they were hugely significant customers to manufacturers.

Department stores were particularly important in developing the direct selling techniques of window and in-store display. By the late 1930s, instead of departments being allocated windows, with dressing the responsibility of department sales staff, a more centralized approach began to be developed with trained display staff employed. For example, in 1946, Eric Lucking was appointed as the first display manager at Liberty's and was responsible for many window displays that helped to revolutionize the selling of merchandise.[14]

4.4 *A display in Lewis's department store, Manchester, 1947.*
AAD/1993/13/4/8/3

4.5 *The fashion department in the Peter Jones department store, 1950.*
With acknowledgement to the
John Lewis Partnership archive collection

Buying and selling

The fashion buyer has been largely neglected by fashion historians, yet their role in the selection of the ready-to-wear available to customers was crucial. Most of the larger stores and chains allocated a fixed budget to a buyer at the beginning of the production season, which was used to buy initial stocks. No additional money was generally available to them for further purchases until a large part of the initial sum had been recovered from sales.[15] To those trying to sell their merchandise, the buyer is often portrayed as a powerful tyrant, dangling substantial budgets but dictating restrictive conditions before confirming any orders. Eric Newby, with a wholesaler's perspective, paints the buyer in such a manner, but also illustrates their role in the selling of ready-to-wear. He recounts the visit of a northern buyer to his father's London wholesale business, Lane and Newby. She received the undivided attention of the staff for a whole day, was plied with treats and then insisted on discussing the 'specials' she would like for her valued customers, before considering placing an order for the company's main merchandise –

ready-to-wear women's suits. The central buyers from the chain stores, even with the prospect of large orders, were seemingly no better. If they did manage to secure a large order from them, Newby claimed it was so constrained by the buyer's conditions that any profit was negligible. While the proprietors of madam shops, sometimes 'set up in business by admirers', might place orders, with such small concerns these were never guaranteed and there was always the added problem of a high number of firms going out of business or changing proprietor.[16]

As a consequence of the increase in branded clothing, a change began to occur in how clothing was sold to the consumer. Particularly in the context of the department store, a trend was seen towards self-service, whereby customers chose items from rails, with swing tags and special displays publicizing specific brands. The advertising of brands contributed to much more knowledgeable customers, who often arrived at a retail outlet with a clear idea of what they were shopping for. Rather than relying on a relationship with a saleswoman skilled in fulfilling an individual customer's tastes and requirements, the increase in branded merchandise reduced the need for trained sales staff (4.5). But a comment from one retailer, in *Fashions and Fabrics' Brand Survey* 1953, suggested that brands were stocked *because* of a 'lack of trained staff'.[17]

Horrockses Fashions and retailers

In order to make a success in the ready-to-wear business, yet retain the notion of exclusivity, it was vital for Horrockses to choose carefully the retailers it supplied. The company avoided downmarket shops and stores, and limited the number of outlets which it supplied in any particular town in order to ensure an area was not flooded with its products. Such strategies were essential if it was going to minimize its mass production status. Maintaining good relations with retailers and their buyers was a high priority and the company concentrated its sales efforts into the seasonal fashion shows held at Hanover Square, with buyers tending to come to Horrockses rather than travelling sales staff visiting retailers around the country (4.6). In the 1940s, there were two main sales staff based at Hanover Square, Mildred Rackham and Marjorie Ritson, who looked after visiting buyers and were responsible for 'going after' large accounts. Expanding business meant that, by 1949, two sales staff was felt to be inadequate and discussions took place to increase their number.[18] A management meeting in 1950 considered the possibility of sending Rackham out to provincial towns with a model and engaging a room in a hotel in order to show the company's garments and secure new customers. It was felt that holiday centres in particular could be targeted.[19] Such strategies were under constant review and James Cleveland Belle often borrowed American selling techniques, including suggesting 'a complete market survey in the home market... in order to establish definitively who the company's customers are'.[20] Horrockses frequently provided retail outlets with display material, including display boards, which linked its merchandise with promotions appearing in magazines such as *Vogue*. In 1950, Horrockses produced 75,000 coloured circulars promoting items from its latest collection, which were to be distributed throughout eight stores 'at a cost of less than £100 each store'.[21]

Horrockses Fashions sold to department stores, to the multiple chains and to independent shops. Accounts with chains and department stores were very important, as they were able to place large orders allowing Horrockses to plan production much more effectively. From 1956 to 1958, Horrockses' largest multiple chain customer was Richard Shops. Between 1956 and 1958, they ordered over 48,000 garments at a value of over £149,000.[22] Other significant customers were Hunts Dress Shops (41,000 garments), Channelle Ltd (37,000), Maryons Fashions (31,000) and Cresta Silks Ltd (22,000).[23] Horrockses also sometimes supplied Dorothy Perkins, but this tended to be with the cheaper styles, or as a means of off-loading out of season stock. Included among its department store customers were Marshall & Snelgrove, Owen Owen,

*4.7 A window in the Manchester
department store Kendal Milne.
The display from 1950 is of
'Cotton in Fashion'.*
Manchester Archives and Local Studies

Bon Marché, Kendal Milne (4.7), Dickins & Jones, Fenwicks and Galeries Lafayette. Considerable business also came from Peter Robinson, Harvey Nichols and D.H. Evans. In order to secure and maintain these accounts, bulk orders were sold to them at discounted rates and 'specials' were made. Horrockses Fashions continued to conduct business with many independent shops even though they were often placing comparatively small orders. Such a practice reflects the fact that they still held a substantial share of the fashion retail business, although this was falling. The availability of Horrockses Fashions' in high-class independents helped the company to promote the idea that it was a superior brand.

It has been established that branding held specific advantages for the manufacturer, but the opinion of retailers was often divided. While some felt that branded merchandise made selling easier, others expressed dissatisfaction about the lack of control that they had over pricing. Goods were usually provided by manufacturers with fixed or suggested retail prices. Often these were included in consumer advertising and retailers complained about the resulting small profit margins.

Retailers were critical of ready-to-wear manufacturers who swamped towns and cities with the same lines. It was in Horrockses' interest to avoid this, as it would compromise the value of exclusivity that it was trying to promote. Although its dresses could be purchased in most major cities and towns in Britain and the colonies (between 1955 and 1958 over 900 outlets in England alone had accounts),[24] the company attempted to select carefully the styles that it sold to each retailer and was particularly vigilant if the brand was sold by more than one outlet in the same town. It was usual for the company to limit the number of retailers it sold to in one location based on a town or city's population. Horrockses frequently refused requests from retailers to carry its brand – often the decision was taken because the order was too small to result in a good return. The names of retailers that appeared in a 1949 list of 200 'Accounts Refused' suggest that the majority of these were madam shops. For example, the two listed from Eastbourne were 'Eve' and 'Winifred Oswald'.[25] Such a practice confirms the complaints received by *Fashions and Fabrics* when it surveyed its readers in 1951.[26]

Sometimes a larger retailer in a city was refused due to the quality and price of goods stocked. In these cases, Horrockses Fashions felt that the reputation of its own brand would be tarnished by association. Potential large accounts were also refused because of adverse reactions from existing customers who feared competition. In 1951, Horrockses decided to refuse to reopen Lewis's account as it was predicted that both Selfridges and Bon Marché would close theirs if they did. In the same year, Helena Ashcroft of Town & Country Clothes, Manchester wrote to the company requesting to be able to stock Horrockses Fashions and its children's brand Pirouette. The request regarding Horrockses Fashions was refused by Herbert Mallott on the grounds that it already had 'an account in close proximity to you in King Street... which was opened with us at the commencement of our Fashion business'. However, Town & Country Clothes was allowed to take Pirouette.[27]

The fostering of the 'exclusive' nature of its product was a deliberate strategy by Horrockses, and is confirmed by one purchaser, Ruth Addison, who recalled the independent retailer Sidney Higginsons in Lytham St Annes, Lancashire. The proprietor made clothes for Ruth and her mother, but also stocked ready-to-wear lines, including Horrockses. The demand for these was so great that Mr Higginson would telephone valued customers when a new stock of Horrockses' dresses came in, so that they could beat the rush![28] The impression that Horrockses' products were difficult to get hold of was implied in an advertisement for Curzons in Australia, which announced that, 'Curzons' Horrockses arrive Tuesday 9.05am. One delivery and one only this year, so stake your "Horrockses" claim early!'.[29]

In order to retain valued retail customers, it was crucial for Horrockses Fashions to maintain the quality of the brand, and to ensure that delivery was timely and coincided with advertising and promotion. Several complaints received from customers about late deliveries were discussed at the company's management meetings. The most serious problem occurred in 1951, and resulted in the company undertaking a major investigation into the reasons why it had not met its delivery promises on the Spring collection. In fact, the company had failed to deliver on time a calamitous 74.5 per cent of the first collection and 40.5 per cent of the second, and it was noted that 'there is no doubt that many of our customers are very bitter about it'.[30]

The range of outlets where Horrockses Fashions' garments could be purchased in any particular location tells us something about the scale of the company's operation and the types of retail outlet it dealt with. For example, in Manchester, the company supplied 11 outlets between 1955 and 1958 when the city's population was 692,200. The outlets included: four department stores (Affleck & Brown, Kendal Milne, Marshall & Snelgrove, and Finnigans Ltd); the chains Cresta Silks Ltd and Robinson & Cleaver; several independent dress shops, including Samuels on King Street, a large upmarket store on three floors, which also had a branch in Hale, Cheshire; and the smaller concerns, Dolores and L.L. Whitehead (see Table 2). The largest order came from Samuels in 1956 with 1,153 units at a value of £4,889. Marshall & Snelgrove ordered 917 units in 1956 at a value of £2,958, while the madam shop Dolores ordered just 126 items at a value of £434. In a smaller city such as Leicester, with a population of 286,000, Horrockses' products sold in two department stores, two chain outlets and one independent; while in Wolverhampton (with a population of 155,400), they retailed in four outlets, and in the market town of Melton Mowbray (population 14,000), they were limited to one independent, Madame Brenda.[31]

Like many other manufacturers, Horrockses Fashions

Table 2 Retailers Supplied by Horrockses Fashions, Manchester (population 692,200).

NAME OF RETAIL OUTLET	ACCOUNT NUMBER	1955/56 (UNITS PURCHASED + TOTAL VALUE IN £)	1956/57 (UNITS PURCHASED + TOTAL VALUE IN £)	1957/58 (UNITS PURCHASED + TOTAL VALUE IN £)
Affleck & Brown	607/A2	397 / £1790	609 / £2341	957 / £3243
A.F. & L. Coulthard	607/C4	- - -	34 / £115	29 / £109
Dolores	607/D3	126 / £434	107 / £423	69 / £320
Cresta Silks Ltd *	607/C1			
Finnigans Ltd	607/F2	204 / £896	8 / £48	- - -
Kendal Milne & Co. Ltd	607/K1	754 / £2809	439 / £2360	426 / £1762
Marshall & Snellgrove	607/M1	917 / £2958	358 / £1213	399 / £965
Robinson & Cleaver *	607/R5			
Samuels	607/S1	1153 / £4889	691 / £3291	613 / £2760
L.L. Whitehead	607/W3	38 / £121	26 / £109	60 / £227
Stanning	607/S4	359 / £1213	116 / £517	183 / £683

* branches of multiple chains were dealt with centrally, so information was recorded collectively, usually by the London branch

had various mutually beneficial arrangements with a number of department stores and chains. For example, bulk orders were sold to retailers at special rates and, in return, examples of Horrockses Fashions' products were used in the retailers own advertising (4.8). Prompt delivery to coincide with such advertisements was paramount. Department stores often organized fashion shows in conjunction with manufacturers of brands and these were publicized locally. One of Horrockses Fashions' first store fashion shows took place in 1947 at Galeries Lafayette in Regent Street, London. This was accompanied by a large window display of Horrockses' merchandise. One employee remembers being instructed to mingle with audience

Colour is lent to this charming group by the gay cotton frocks made by Horrockses for

Lillywhites in many attractive spring shades.   On the *left*, £4.1.11d.   On the *right*, £4.7.5d.

Sizes 12-16.   The tennis dress is of

white tricoline at £6.9.4d. and the

coat of heavy white rayon at £7.7.11d.

Lillywhites
LTD

154

Cotton—cool and colourful

*Two examples from our collections of summer
housegowns by Horrockses. On the left, a strikingly
beautiful pattern of black roses on yellow, pink,
blue, or green grounds. £6.17.0*
*On the right, a bayardère print of colourful roses in
cyclamen/blue/green, yellow/pink/navy, or
turquoise/green/rust on white grounds. £6.14.0*
Both styles in sizes 32 to 38 ins. bust.

*Please state second choice of colour when
ordering by post. We regret no approval.*

Knightsbridge, S.W.1

4.9 Woollands of Knightsbridge
advertises Horrockses' housecoats.
The Queen, 9 May 1951

4.10 A 1947 advertisement for Harvey Nichols
showing a Horrockses' rayon jersey dress designed
exclusively for the store. It retailed at £15.1s.11d.
Vogue, May 1947

4.11 An advertisement from 1952
for a Horrockses' printed poplin
evening gown, exclusive to
Harvey Nichols.
Vogue, May 1952

members to gauge their reaction to the collection, which she recalled was extremely favourable.[32] Styles from the Spring collection of 1954 were shown in the Pump Rooms, Bath in conjunction with the chain store Maryons, and compèred by television personality Eamon Andrews.[33]

Horrockses would produce specials for certain retailers, which meant that the style or fabric used was exclusive to a particular store. Such a practice often resulted in the store advertising the line (4.9). Horrockses had a long-standing arrangement of this kind with Harvey Nichols in London and with the Cresta chain (4.10, 4.11). Specials were also produced for provincial department stores such as Daly's of Glasgow and

Horrockses evening dress in fine printed poplin. Primrose with cornflower predominating. grey/cerise, orchid/citron or powder blue/carnation pink. hip sizes 36—42 14½ gns

HARVEY NICHOLS
of Knightsbridge

Harvey Nichols & Co., Ltd., Knightsbridge, London, S.W.1. Sloane 5440

4.12 Horrockses sold
in many provincial
department stores,
including Daly's of
Glasgow. Here the store
advertises two examples
of its stock of Horrockses
Fashions products.
Vogue, March 1951

156

Horrockses cottons

at

*This attractive style in more tailored lines
is available in a variety of colours
Sizes 14 to 18.   £5 . 16 . 3 including postage
Shoes by RAYNE*

*Multi-coloured sun-dress and matching bolero
Sizes 12, 14, 16.   £6 . 8 . 0 including postage
Regret no approval*

Dalys

of Scotland

DALY & SONS LTD SAUCHIEHALL STREET GLASGOW C 2

4.13 This advertisement highlights the notion of
'Britishness' and the Horrockses Fashions' product,
as a means of attracting foreign customers.
Vogue Book of British Export, no.6, 1948

4.14 Constance Morris on holiday
in Nice, 1958.
Mrs C. Morris

Schofield's of Leeds (4.12). However, a fine balance had to be maintained between satisfying individual retailers' requirements and production efficiency. The 1951 investigation noted that one of the issues that had resulted in late deliveries was that store buyers were insisting on stipulating their own choice of colours and sizes. This had complicated the situation and London sales staff were subsequently urged to encourage their customers to order in assorted colours and sizes.[34]

Exports were a key part of the Horrockses Fashions' operation and the garments sold in significant quantities abroad, often promoted as a quality British product, in a limited range of outlets (4.13). The company was particularly successful in Germany, Scandinavia, Belgium, Holland and Switzerland. In New York, Horrockses' clothing graced the windows of Altman's, who advertised the arrival of the company in 1955: 'A new collection of these beautiful cotton dresses (imported from England and only at Altman's) is a great event on our third floor. Made of superb quality fabrics… they're finished with fastidious British attention to detail'. Altman's noted that '…they are made in England and clamoured for on the Continent. Because of the demand, B. Altman here has recently put its collection of Horrockses in a special corner of our dress department'.[35] The dresses were sold in outlets in Commonwealth countries and Kurt Lowit said that, when travelling abroad, 'you could always tell an Englishwoman by her Horrockses dress' (4.14).[36]

This cotton frock by Horrockses, in sizes
11. 12, 13, 14, 16 and 18, costs £4 18 7
and seven coupons.
Regret no approval but patterns of material
available on request.   Postage 1/6 extra.

Dalys OF SCOTLAND

DALY & SONS LTD   SAUCHIEHALL STREET · GLASGOW C2

4.15 This bayadere print is used for a full-skirted button-through dress, in an advertisement for Daly's department store. Horrockses Fashions continued to produce some of its fashions under the Utility Scheme until it ended in 1952.
Vogue, March 1949

4.16 A promotional photograph showing typists in Horrockses, Crewdson & Co.'s Preston office, 1954. The majority are wearing Horrockses Fashions' garments. They were able to purchase unsold stock at the end of the season for £1.
Wendy Simpson

4.17 Kitty Black and friend wearing Horrockses Fashions' outfits in a photograph for Picture Post, 1954.
Jack Esten

The Horrockses Fashions' customer

The Horrockses' customer is difficult to classify. At one extreme, Horrockses' products were worn by the 'great and the good', as evidenced by the list of names in the surviving measurement book: royalty, fashion journalists, film and stage actresses, and even the directrice of the House of Balmian in Paris, Ginette Spanier. But, at the other end of the spectrum, Horrockses' garments were purchased by women on modest incomes, who saved hard-earned cash in order to be able to buy one outfit. The cost of a Horrockses' dress suggests that the typical purchaser was a reasonably well-off middle-class woman, and certainly the majority interviewed fall into this

category (4.17). Retail prices for Horrockses' garments varied, starting at about £4 to £5 for a simple cotton shirtwaister and rising to £15 for a poplin full-length evening dress.[37] The prices were comparable to labels such as Linzi and Sambo, but more expensive than Horrockses, Crewdson & Co.'s Reybro brand (at just over £2 for a cotton dress), or Marks & Spencer and C&A. But the assumption that only middle-class women purchased the outfits is a simplistic one and income is not necessarily an indication of an individual's purchasing preferences (4.16). There are many different attitudes to spending on fashion and it is clear from interviews with some Horrockses' customers that, while many were well off (4.18, 4.19), there were others whose

4.18 Gill Jones (centre) pictured at an Oxford University summer ball c.1955–6, when she was a student nurse. She purchased her evening dress with its design of irises at a branch of the chain Channelle, in Oxford.

Gill Jones

4.19 The evening dress worn by Gill Jones in 4.18, c.1955–6.

Courtesy of the Harris Museum and Art Gallery, Preston:
PRSMG: 2005.38
Photograph by Norwyn Ltd

4.20 This summer dress was purchased by Jean Moffatt in 1959 from the department store Brown & Muff in Bradford for a garden party at the school where she had just started her first teaching job.
Christine Boydell
Photograph by Nigel Essex

desire to own a Horrockses' dress led them to scrimp and save to purchase just one. Jean Moffatt bought a full-skirted Horrockses' summer dress in 1959 from the department store Brown & Muff in Bradford for a garden party at the school where she had just started her first teaching job (4.20). She remembers thinking the dress was very expensive and, with a salary of £37 per month, she had to think long and hard before purchasing it. Eventually, though, she decided to buy and it became one of her favourite dresses.[38]

Customers were motivated by a combination of factors when choosing to purchase a Horrockses' dress: most mention fabric, colour, cotton and styling (4.21, 4.22). The quality of

4.21 *A bow detail on a Horrockses'
cotton summer dress.*
V&A: T.673-1996

4.22 *A sundress and bolero printed
with a design of plates of food.*
Courtesy of Harris Museum
and Art Gallery, Preston:
PRSMG: 2001.37
Photograph by Norwyn Ltd

4.23 Ann Parr bought this
Horrockses Fashions' sundress
and bolero in 1953 from
Bourne & Hollingsworth on
Regent Street, London.
Ann Parr

4.24 Underarm construction of
a Horrockses' dress illustrating
the firm's attention to detail in
the making-up process.
Courtesy of Harris Museum
and Art Gallery, Preston:
PRSMG: 2000.308

cloth was part of the appeal, as Ruth Addison commented, 'The cottons were so fine and soft, that's why they were so nice'.[39] The colours were also singled out. Joyce Beaumont remembered a dress she had '... in a gorgeous shade of coffee, a light shade – oh it was a gorgeous dress in a beautiful poplin material'. She recalled the sensation of wearing the voluminous skirts and how wonderful it was to walk down the streets 'with all the swishing'.[40] The clarity and attractive nature of the printed designs were commented on, though it would appear that the women who bought the dresses were unaware of the patterns' origins, choosing particular designs (especially florals and stripes) simply because they liked them (4.26). In 1953, when she was 18, Ann Parr bought a Horrockses Fashions'

sundress and bolero from Bourne & Hollingsworth on Regent Street (4.23). She had no idea that the print had been designed by Eduardo Paolozzi, but chose it as it was the first thing she saw that 'got me very excited, because it suddenly felt I was experiencing exciting times and it seemed like a design for the future'. She had other Horrockses Fashions' dresses, but felt that this one stood out 'as being different'.[41]

Although expensive, Horrockses Fashions' garments were considered by many who wore them to be good value for money. The fact that they were 'well-made' (a frequent phrase used) and of quality cotton meant they stayed looking good year after year (4.24, 4.25). Irenie Ashwin-Nayler, who had just returned from an extensive tour of the Middle East in 1953, was

4.25 *A cotton shirtwaister with detail.*
Courtesy of Harris Museum
and Art Gallery, Preston:
PRSMG: 1999.562.1.
Photograph by Norwyn Ltd

4.26 *A green-striped button-through dress in lightweight cotton; the fabric design also came in grey, yellow, mauve and pink colourways. The dress was illustrated in a Jenners' catalogue of Spring 1955, with a retail price of 4½ guineas.*
Christine Boydell.
Photograph by Nigel Essex.

4.27 The fashion salon in Kendal
Milne, Manchester, 1956,
illustrating the store's maintenance
of a personal approach to selling.
Manchester Archives and Local Studies

so impressed with the product that she wrote to Horrockses complimenting them on the durability of their dresses. She mentioned the 'primitive' conditions she had encountered and the fact that her clothes were washed in rivers and 'slashed against stones', and because of the heat they required frequent laundering. She had three Horrockses' dresses and, while most of her other clothes were ruined by the end of the trip, she commented that 'the Horrockses dresses were good as new, and in perfect condition'.[42]

Women's experience of shopping for Horrockses Fashions' products varied, with many buying from a town or city centre department store and some buying from local

4.28 Elizabeth Arrowsmith in Bombay in 1951 en route to Malaya, in a pale green, pink and white dress.
Elizabeth Arrowsmith

4.29 Elizabeth Arrowsmith photographed in Malaya in 1951 wearing a green and white striped Horrockses' dress. Many purchasers commented on how perfect such dresses were for a hot climate.
Elizabeth Arrowsmith

independent retailers. Lesley Blackledge recalled shopping with her mother at N&E Maidens, a small independent shop in Chorley, Lancashire.[43] She remembered Miss Maiden ringing to say 'I've got a Horrockses, Miss Blackledge, which is just your thing'. This personal touch was typical of the madam shop and is mentioned by many women shopping for clothes in the 1940s and '50s. In addition, if an outfit did not fit perfectly, madam shops would alter it for the customer. This practice illustrates that an element of customization was still required by consumers even though they were buying ready-to-wear. High-class department stores also attempted to maintain a personal approach. Lesley's mother-in-law sometimes shopped at Marshall & Snelgrove in Manchester. Here, she would be given a chair and dresses were brought to her, and if she wished she could take them home on approval and have them altered if necessary (4.27). Some women refer to the style of selling in such stores as 'hover and pounce'. Veronica McEvoy described this as the favoured approach of the department store Finnigans in Manchester.[44] She found this off-putting and preferred the less pressured approach of

Kendal Milne or Affleck & Brown, where she purchased two Horrockses' dresses in the mid-1950s.

The memories and experiences of specific customers coincide with the values and ideals that Horrockses Fashions was trying to promote in its products and there seems to be a consensus that women who purchased a Horrockses' dress were acquiring something special. Elizabeth Arrowsmith described her purchases as 'cotton bliss' (4.28). She bought four dresses and a housecoat as part of her wardrobe for a two-year stay in Malaya, where her husband worked as a civil engineer from 1951 to 1952 (4.29). The cotton was ideal for the climate and she felt that the 'dresses improved with age'. She considered Horrockses Fashions' outfits to be 'really something very special' and remembered the compliments she received when wearing them. So fond was she of her first Horrockses' dress, a blue and white check, that she eventually cut it down and wore it as a skirt.[45]

Ruth Addison first encountered Horrockses' products as a teenager shopping locally with her mother in Lytham St Annes, and on trips to Manchester and London in the early 1950s.

4.30 *Ruth Addison on holiday in
South Africa in the early 1950s,
wearing a Horrockses Fashions'
sundress.*
Ruth Addison

The family were well off and she owned several Horrockses Fashions' garments, including a full-length cotton evening dress. She did not consider them to be very expensive but felt they were quite 'up-market'. Her particular memory is of the quality of the cottons which 'were so different from all the hard cottons that we'd had before. They weren't so nice to wear because they were stiff'. Several Horrockses' dresses were purchased at Sidney Higginsons in Lytham St Annes, which was the only shop in the town were they could be bought; her impression was that they 'weren't plentiful'. She describes this independent shop as 'very up-to-date' and, as well as selling ready-to-wear, he would copy the latest French fashions, which customers picked from a style book. Her experience of buying

at Higginsons illustrates the survival of a personalized way of selling – a special, almost theatrical, event:

> *I remember in St Annes. They drew the curtains across,
> you couldn't just go in and look, you had to ask and then
> the curtain was drawn back and they showed you what
> they wanted you to see, until, when you knew them very
> well you'd ask if you could just have a look yourself.*[46]

Addison describes her experience of shopping in London at Fenwicks and Dickins & Jones as being similar. Horrockses Fashions' garments were often purchased for foreign travel, for honeymoons and other special occasions (4.31). Like many of

4.31 Constance Morris on holiday
in the South of France in 1958, in
a sundress. The matching bolero is
next to her.
Mrs C. Morris

her contemporaries, Addison bought a number of Horrockses' dresses for trips abroad to South America and South Africa, and felt that they were ideal for hot climates, although the volume of fabric in the skirts made them difficult to pack (4.30).

Addison was probably a fairly typical customer. But the experience of Peggy Rimmer demonstrates how a working-class woman could go to unusual lengths to acquire a Horrockses' dress.[47] As a teenager in the early 1950s, Rimmer worked on the family's milk round and around the house, helping to look after her seven younger siblings. Rather than receiving a wage, she was given money when she needed something and occasionally her mother treated her to a dress. That was how she acquired her two Horrockses' outfits, a

shirtwaister and a sundress (4.32, 4.33). She remembered choosing them because they were so nice, particularly the cotton, and she thought that later they could be altered and made into skirts.

Beth Hartley's experience illustrates how women who could not afford a Horrockses Fashions' original could acquire the look by copying the style (4.34). Hartley worked as an office junior in 1947, earning £1.2s.6d. a week. A few years later, as a qualified shorthand typist, her wage had risen to £7.10s. But she felt a Horrockses' dress was beyond her pocket. Instead she used her dressmaking skills to create her own version. In 1954, she bought some Horrockses' material on Preston market and made two summer dresses to take on holiday

4.32 Peggy Rimmer photographed outside Tarleton Church of England Primary School, Lancashire, 1951–2.

Peggy Rimmer

4.33 This dress, in a fabric designed by Alastair Morton (see 2.32), was given to Peggy Rimmer in 1951, in lieu of wages when she worked on the family milk round.

Peggy Rimmer

4.34 *A page from a 1953 book of draftings for home-dressmakers.*

G.A. Haslam, Illustrated Book of Draftings: Spring and Summer Coronation Number 23

For Coronation Gaiety

DRAFTING REFERENCES and
MATERIALS SUGGESTED

FIG. 5
Draftings are on pages 2 and 3.
Printed Silk, Linen, or Silk Jersey.
4/4½ yards 36-in.

FIG. 6
Draftings are on pages 3 and 5.
Printed Silk, Cotton, or Silk Jersey.
4 yards 36-in.

FIG. 7
Draftings are on pages 1 and 5.
Floral Cotton or Silk Jersey.
4/4½ yards 36-in.

FIG. 8
Draftings are on page 1.
Seersucker, Striped Cotton, or
Printed Rayon. 4½ yards 36-in.

4.35 This early 1950s housecoat
is made of cotton printed with
a dramatic design of blue irises.
Christine Boydell. Photograph by Nigel Essex

to Cornwall and remembered 'I felt like the bees-knees in them' (4.36).[48]

The women interviewed often commented that Horrockses Fashions' products were difficult to get hold of and that they were special. This coincides with the impression Horrockses wanted to convey and supports its retail strategy of considering carefully which outlets sold its merchandise. The appeal of the Horrockses' dress in the view of those who bought and wore them lay in the quality and quantity of the fabric and the attention to styling, with the cut and fall of the full-skirted dresses often mentioned. Customers recall that the return to a more feminine shape after the war was met with relief and many women single out Horrockses Fashions' dresses as personifying this look, accessorized with a pair of Joyce shoes and a smart hat. Horrockses Fashions hit the market just at the right time, when women were ready for a taste of luxury, glamour and femininity (4.35). However, there was still a desire for value for money and quality manufacture, as well as durability and practicality. Horrockses Fashions' products seemed to fit the bill perfectly and the company's success in communicating the values of the brand is borne out by the testimonies of the women who bought the dresses, and in this comment from fashion journalist Alison Settle, 'To Horrockses, women owe a deep debt because they caused cotton patterns to grow up and, within the last few years, produced inexpensive clothes of vast distinction' (4.37).[49]

The success of mass-produced fashion was acknowledged

4.36 Beth Hartley on holiday in St Ives Cornwall in 1955, wearing a home-made cotton dress in a Horrockses, Crewdson & Co. fabric.
Beth Hartley

4.37 Left to right: Christine Haigh, Pat Bennett, Anne Shackleton and Juliet Leeson on holiday at Rustington Lido in 1955, when they were all 18. Anne's was a genuine Horrockses' dress, while according to Juliet hers was a 'would-be Horrockses', which was cheaper and purchased from C&A in Leeds. Christine's dress was home-made.
Juliet Amery (née Leeson)

4.38 The Duchess of Kent in a striped cotton shirtwaister, one of 10 Horrockses Fashions' outfits that she chose for her 1952 tour of the Far East.
William Parrott, The Pictorial Story of The HRH The Duchess of Kent's Far East Tour with HRH The Duke of Kent: an Eye Witness Account

4.39 Pauline Altham and Helen Johnston (fashion designer for Horrockses Pirouette) photographed in 1952–3. Pauline wears an identical dress to the one modelled by Barbara Goalen in 4.40 and the Duchess of Kent in 4.38.
Christine Boydell

4.40 Barbara Goalen models a button-through version of the dress chosen by the Duchess of Kent.
Vogue, June 1952

by *Vogue* magazine in 1951, when it announced that now 'the most fastidious and fashion-conscious woman can dress immaculately for any occasion in ready-to-wear clothes'.[50] The purchase of a Horrockses' ready-made dress not only provided this possibility, but also, for the first time in the history of fashion, an ordinary customer had the opportunity to purchase identical dresses to those worn by royalty and the top models of the day (4.38, 4.39, 4.40). Horrockses' success in communicating the message that its cotton fashions were exclusive and special meant that the clothes were desired by many, while the reasonable price tag allowed large numbers of women to purchase them. But the climate was changing. By the

Horrockses Fashions
in Fine Cotton

late 1950s, British cotton firms faced increasing competition from the Far East and from the man-made fibres industry, which resulted in the parent company instigating increasing cost-cutting strategies, including a reduction in the quality of the cotton cloth made available to Horrockses Fashions. This and other compromises lead to the resignation of some of the company's key players: James Cleveland Belle left in 1958, followed by Kurt Lowit and Pat Albeck. By 1964, Horrockses, Crewdson & Co. could no longer see the promotional value of owning a fashion business and sold Horrockses Fashions to Steinberg & Sons (owners of the Alexon brand), who secured a Royal Warrant for the label in the same year. It survived until 1983, largely on a reputation built up between 1946 and 1958. Increasingly, synthetic fibres overtook cotton and the transfer of clothing production to the Far East exacerbated a decline in quality (4.41).

The launch of a ready-to-wear label by Horrockses, Crewdson & Co. as a means of promoting its cotton cloth was well timed. The wartime regulation of clothing production meant that the industry emerged from the Second World War better organized, more efficient and in an improved position to meet the exacting demands of post-war customers for good quality ready-to-wear fashions. Horrockses benefited from these developments and the strategic promotion of cotton by the Cotton Board also proved advantageous. Horrockses Fashions' effective promotional strategies, emphasizing the

4.42 *A sketch of a dress (style 756), with a sample fabric attached, c.1952. This style is very similar to one of the Horrockses' Dresses chosen by the Duchess of Kent.*

Daphne Razzell (née Patten)

exclusivity and glamour of the brand, were balanced against the realities of ready-to-wear production (4.42). The company was able to produce in quantity, well-designed fashions – using quality cottons in original patterns – that were reasonably priced. The esteem in which Horrockses Fashions' products were held by the women who purchased them is testament to the company's success in achieving its aim to 'bring quality goods of our own manufacture before the public'.[51]

This study of Horrockses Fashions has illuminated the entire cycle involved in the production of ready-to-wear fashion garments, from initial concept to end use by the customer. It has highlighted the relationship between cloth, fabric design and fashion styling; the importance of branding and promotion and their impact on the Horrockses' customer; and the changing role of the retailer in the distribution of fashionable dress. Such an approach acknowledges the hybrid nature of fashion and responds to Joanne Entwistle's plea 'that new studies on fashion and dress need to address the interconnections between production and consumption'.[52] This book provides an important contribution to an understanding of everyday dress so often neglected in favour of discussions of couture fashion.

Ivy Mill No.

London Ref. No. 456.

as 563

Cloth No. 16750.

EVERGLAZE
ONLY

Notes

Introduction
'Horrockses Fashions':
A New Ready-to-Wear Label

1. P.J. Reynolds, 'Cool Crisp Cottons',
    Country Life (10 May 1946), p.874
2. 'Cotton is the New Fabric for Fashion',
    Evening Standard (28 March 1946)
    (LRO: DDHs 49/1 1940–46 Newscuttings Book)
3. 'Cotton Concerto', *The Drapers' Record*
    (13 April 1946), pp.46–7
4. In 1946, when Pauline Altham began working for
    Horrockses Fashions in London as an assistant to the
    sample room manager, she earned £3 per week, rising to
    £8 when she left in 1953. Daphne Patten began at the
    firm in 1946 as an illustrator earning £2 per week; by the
    time she left in 1954, she was assistant to the fashion
    designer John Tullis and her wage had risen to £10.
5. *Inaugural Presentation of Fashions in Cotton*, 1946
    (AAD/1995/16/12/1)

Chapter One
Exclusivity Off-the-Peg

1. *The Ipswich Journal* (15 June 1844), issue 4487
2. 'Specialities', *The Ladies Treasury* (1 March 1887), p.177
3. T.M. Brookes, 'Horrockses, Crewdson & Co. High
    Quality of Products Maintained', *The Times*
    (2 January 1947), p.7
4. *Film Fashionland* (November 1934), p.2
5. T.M. Brookes, 'Horrockses, Crewdson & Co.
    New Northern Ireland Factory', *The Times*
    (7 January 1948), p.9
6. 'Cotton into Fashion: the Romance of Horrockses',
    Fashions and Fabrics Overseas (1954), no.2, p.56
7. Wray (1957), p.23
8. Ibid., p.25
9. Ewing (1974), p.142
10. Wray (1957), p.46
11. Reynolds (1995), p.57
12. Garland (1970), p.38
13. Reynolds (1995), p.13
14. Wray (1957), p.55
15. Ibid., p.53
16. Director's report for the year ending 31 August 1946
    (LRO: DDVC Acc 7340 Box 22/2)
17. Interview with Pauline Altham (née Read), July 2008

18. The size 14 referred to is small compared to today's
    sizing and is equivalent to a contemporary size 10 or 12.
19. Wray (1957), p.195
20. Investigation into failure of Horrockses Fashions
    to carry out delivery promises, 1951
    (LRO: DDVC Acc 7340 Box 12/3)
21. Memorandum from Mr Leadbetter to Mr Gaskell,
    30 January 1948 (LRO: DDVC Acc 7340 Box 12/4)
22. 'Obituary Mr J. Cleveland Belle', *The Times*
    (26 August 1983), p.10
23. Interview with Pauline Altham (née Read), May 2009
24. Interview with Daphne Razzell (née Patten),
    November 2009
25. Letter to the author from Virginia McKenna,
    19 June 2008
26. Horrockses Fashions Limited. Extract from Verbatim
    Report of the Management Meeting, 31 August 1949
    (LRO: DDVC Acc 7340 Box 12/3)
27. Horrockses Fashions Limited. Extract from Verbatim
    Report of the Management Meeting, 31 October 1951
    (LRO: DDVC Acc 7340 Box 12/3)
28. Investigation into failure of Horrockses Fashions
    to carry out delivery promises, 1951
    (LRO: DDVC Acc 7340 Box 12/3)
29. Horrockses Fashions Limited. Extract from Verbatim
    Report of the Management Meeting, 27 June 1951
    (LRO: DDVC Acc 7340 Box 12/3)
30. Analysis of production and sales, 25 July 1952
    (LRO: DDVC Acc 7340 Box 13/3)
31. Horrockses Fashions Limited. Extract from Verbatim
    Report of the Management Meeting, 7 June 1950
    (LRO: DDVC Acc 7340 Box 12/3)
32. Letter from Mr J. Fletcher to Mr Kerr, 10 January 1951
    (LRO: DDVC Acc 7340 Box 3/4). Both worked at Ivy
    Mill where Kerr was general manager
33. Horrockses Fashions Limited. Extract from Verbatim
    Report of the Management Meeting, 31 August 1949
    (LRO: DDVC Acc 7340 Box 12/3)
34. Ivy Mill Reports, 26 September 1952
    (LRO: DDVC Acc 7340 Box 13/3)
35. Ibid. Other companies used included Holsteads
    and Tunstall (mainly for children's wear), Arbee
    Gowns of Northampton, Almo Gowns,
    Chatsworth and Fergusons.

36. On her return to Australia, Gloria Smythe enjoyed a
    successful career as a designer for Speedo.
37. Director's report for the year ending 31 August 1948
    (LRO: DDVC Acc 7340 Box 22/2)
38. Information provided by Bernard Leser (managing
    director of Horrockses Fashions (Canada), 1952–6).
39. T.M. Brookes, 'Horrockses, Crewdson & Co. Home Sales
    Volume Maintained', *The Times* (20 December 1956), p.17
40. Horrockses Fashions Limited. Extract from Verbatim
    Report of the Management Meeting, 25 January 1950
    (LRO: DDVC Acc 7340 Box 12/3)
41. Horrockses Fashions Limited. Extract from Verbatim
    Report of the Management Meeting, 26 October 1949
    (LRO: DDVC Acc 7340 Box 12/3)
42. Investigation into failure of Horrockses Fashions
    to carry out delivery promises, 1951
    (LRO: DDVC Acc 7340 Box 12/3)
43. 'Garments of Gladness', *The Overseas Daily Mail*
    (13 April 1946) (DDHs 49/1 1940–46
    Newscuttings Book)

Chapter Two
'In Fine Cotton': Fabric and Fashion

1. Audrey Withers, 'Fashion, Dress Fabrics and Accessories', *Design '46* (London, 1946), p.45
2. Lesley E. Miller, 'Perfect Harmony: Textile Manufacturers and Haute Couture 1947–57', *The Golden Age of Couture: Paris and London 1947–57* (London, 2007), ch.5
3. Lou Taylor, 'De-coding the Hierarchy of Fashion Textiles', *Disentangling Textiles: Techniques for the Study of Designed Objects* (London, 2002), pp.67–80
4. Mendes and Hinchcliffe (1987)
5. Wray (1957), p.23
6. Ibid., p.54
7. Amy de la Haye, 'The Dissemination of Design From Haute Couture to Fashionable Ready-to-Wear During the 1920s', *Textile History* (1993), vol.24, no.1, p.44
8. 'Cotton is the New Fabric for Fashion', *Evening Standard* (28 March 1946) (LRO: DDHs 49/1)
9. 'Cotton that is Different', *Imperial Review* (June 1946) (DDHs 49/1 1940–46 Newscuttings Book)
10. G.E. Moggridge, 'The Colour, Design and Style Centre', *Art and Industry* (1956), vol.60, no.358, pp.110–17
11. Anthea Jarvis, 'British Cotton Couture', *Costume* (1997), no.31, pp.92–9
12. Donald Tomlinson, 'Promoting Cotton in Wholesale and High Fashion', *Design* (1952), no.42, pp.4–9
13. Miller (2007), pp.128–9
14. Horrockses Fashions Limited. Extract from Verbatim Report of the Management Meeting, 25 May 1949 (LRO: DDVC Acc 7340 Box 12/3)
15. Horrockses Fashions Limited. Extract from Verbatim Report of the Management Meeting, 30 November 1949 (LRO: DDVC Acc 7340 Box 12/3)
16. *Sunday Times* (15 June 1952) (DDHs 49/1 1940–46 Newscuttings Book)
17. Pevsner (1937), p.48
18. Horrockses Fashions Limited. Extract from Verbatim Report of the Management Meeting, 29 March 1950 (LRO: DDVC Acc 7340 Box 12/3)
19. Quoted in Horrockses Fashions Limited. Extract from Verbatim Report of the Management Meeting, 30 November 1949 (LRO: DDVC Acc 7340 Box 12/3)
20. Interview with Marny Shorrocks (née Tickle), January 2008
21. Interview with Joyce Badrocke, October 2008

22. Horrockses Fashions Limited. Extract from Verbatim Report of the Management Meeting, 27 July 1949 (LRO: DDVC Acc 7340 Box 12/3)
23. Pevsner (1937), p.58
24. Lecture to a Design and Industries Association meeting for retail buyers and salesmen in Manchester, 13 December 1938 (Scottish Records Office: GD326-164)
25. Agreement re payments to Alastair Morton (LRO: DDVC Acc Box 12/4)
26. 'Britain Marshals her Design Talent', *Fashions and Fabrics Overseas* (January–February 1949), p.94
27. The hypotrochoid curves are created by rolling one circle inside a stationary circle, as in the classic toy Spirograph.
28. Horrockses Fashions Limited. Extract from Verbatim Report of the Management Meeting, 27 July 1949 (LRO: DDVC Acc 7340 Box 12/3)
29. Ibid.
30. Letter from Alastair Morton to Mr Leadbetter, 29 May 1955 (LRO: DDVC Acc Box 12/4)
31. 'Britain Marshals her Design Talent', *Fashions and Fabrics Overseas* (January–February 1949), p.94
32. Christine Boydell, 'Pat Albeck: Textile Designs for Horrockses Fashions Limited 1953–58', *Text* (2001–2), vol.29, pp.5–9
33. Geoffrey Rayner et al., *Artists' Textiles in Britain 1945–1970* (London, 2003)
34. Nikolaus Pevsner, 'Can Painters Design Fabrics?', *Harpers Bazaar* (November 1945), p.13
35. Mendes and Hinchcliffe (1987), pp.102–3
36. Horrockses Fashions Limited. Extract from Verbatim Report of the Management Meeting, 27 July 1949 (LRO: DDVC Acc 7340 Box 12/3)
37. Horrockses Fashions Limited. Extract from Verbatim Report of the Management Meeting, 31 August 1949 (LRO: DDVC Acc 7340 Box 12/3)
38. 'Pattern in Contrast', *The Ambassador* (1955), no.10, pp.100–125
39. My thanks to Louis and Pierre le Brocquy for this information.
40. Correspondence from Herbert Mallott to W. Rondas, 17 October 1951 (LRO: DDVC Acc 7340 Box 3/1)
41. The George Ainscow Archive is held by the Archive of Art & Design (AAD/1993/12/1/1)
42. Boydell (2001–2), p.6. A *croquis* was the name given to a sketch not in repeat.

43. Letter to the author from Sir Terence Conran, October 2008
44. Horrockses Fashions Limited. Extract from Verbatim Report of the Management Meeting, 25 January 1950 (LRO: DDVC Acc 7340 Box 12/3)
45. Horrockses Fashions Limited. Extract from Verbatim Report of the Management Meeting, 29 March 1950 (LRO: DDVC Acc 7340 Box 12/3)
46. Correspondence with Bernard Leser, 22 April 2009
47. Interview with Stephanie Houlgrave (née Godfrey), November 2000
48. Horrockses Fashions Limited. Extract from Verbatim Report of the Management Meeting, 6 August 1951 (LRO: DDVC Acc 7340 Box 12/3)
49. Horrockses Fashions Limited. Extract from Verbatim Report of the Management Meeting, 26 April 1950 (LRO: DDVC Acc 7340 Box 12/3)
50. Interview with Stephanie Houlgrave (née Godfrey), November 2000
51. Horrockses Fashions Limited. Extract from Verbatim Report of the Management Meeting, 29 June 1949 (LRO: DDVC Acc 7340 Box 12/3)
52. Horrockses Fashions Limited. Extract from Verbatim Report of the Management Meeting, 31 August 1949 (LRO: DDVC Acc 7340 Box 12/3)
53. Horrockses Fashions Limited. Extract from Verbatim Report of the Management Meeting, 28 February 1951 (LRO: DDVC Acc 7340 Box 12/3)
54. Telephone interview with Joe David, October 2008

Chapter Three
'Horrockses Fashions': Promoting the Brand

1. Wray (1957), pp.136–7. The percentage is made up from the total number of branded clothing items listed annually in the *Fashions and Fabrics: Branded Merchandise and Trade Marks Directory*.

2. Ibid., p.134

3. Director's report for the year ending 31 August 1944 (LRO: DDVC Acc 7340 Box 22/2)

4. Horrockses Fashions Limited. Extract from Verbatim Report of the Management Meeting, 31 August 1949 (LRO: DDVC Acc 7340 Box 12/3)

5. *Horse & Hound* (22 October 1887), p.639

6. Newby (1970,) p.210

7. 'Retailers are Looking More Critically at Branded Merchandise', *Fashions and Fabrics* (August 1952), p.33

8. *Fashions and Fabrics* began an annual 'Survey of Brands' in 1949, in an effort to establish the extent of branding in Britain and the reactions to it by their readers.

9. 'Analysis of "You didn't have it"', *Fashions and Fabrics* (April 1952), p.75

10. Ibid. (August 1953), p.40

11. Ibid. (August 1952), p.33

12. Lord Hollenden, 'Brands: the Best Insurance of Quality', *Fashions and Fabrics: Branded Merchandise and Trade Marks Directory* (1955), p.v

13. Walter Lea, 'Five Year Advertising Plan Mooted for Leicester', *The Drapers' Record* (21 December 1946), p.14

14. Wray (1957), p.145

15. A British export journal, edited by Hans Juda. It was extremely forward looking and a great supporter of Horrockses Fashions.

16. The export arm of *Fashions and Fabrics* (formally *The Drapers' Organiser*).

17. Dawnay (1956), p.13

18. Wray (1957), p.138

19. Horrockses Fashions Limited. Extract from Verbatim Report of the Management Meeting, 6 August 1951 (LRO: DDVC Acc 7340 Box 12/3)

20. Figures based on 'Schedule of Final Costings for the 1952 Spring Collection' (LRO: DDVC Acc 7340 Box 13/3)

21. Minutes of R.H. Reynolds Brothers Limited, 28 June 1950 (LRO: DDVC Acc 7340 Box 27/5)

22. Observations on the 1950s season and suggestions for 1951 (LRO: DDVC Acc 7340 Box 12/3)

23. *The Tatler* (22 May 1946) (LRO: DDHs 49/1 1940–46 Newscuttings Book)

24. 'Measurements *Record*', Gloria Smythe, *1952–1956* (92/1728-21), Powerhouse Museum, Sydney, Australia. My thanks to Gloria Smythe for drawing my attention to this unpublished notebook.

25. *Empire News* (3 August and 21 September 1952) (LRO: DDHs 49/2 1952–55 Newscuttings Book). In fact, the heads of these stars were superimposed on the dresses.

26. 'Measurements *Record*', Gloria Smythe, *1952–1956*. Smythe was John Tullis's assistant and the book lists his special clients. There is evidence that the other fashion designers, Betty Newmarch and Marta Pirn, also had special clients. A measurement book survives in the Betty Newmarch Archive (AAD/1995/16) although this item is not available to researchers.

27. Hugh Beresford, 'Millinery – Film Tie-up', *The Drapers' Record* (19 April 1947), p.2

28. Margaret Disher, 'The Evolution of the "Tie-up" Promotion', *The Maker-up* (May 1953), p.338

29. For example, in *Picture Show and Film Pictorial* (9 August 1952) (LRO: DDHs 49/2 1952–55 Newscuttings Book)

30. Letter to Brian Paxton-White, North West Area Publicist for General Film Distributors, 2 January 1952 (DDVC Acc 7340 Box 3/4)

31. Gwen Brooks, 'Spot the Queen's Dress', *Daily Mirror* (27 November 1953) (LRO: DDHs 49/2 1952–55 Newscuttings Book)

32. 'High Court of Justice, Queen's Bench Division, Libel Action Regarding the Queen's Dresses Settled. Horrockses, Crewdson & Co. Ltd v Associated Newspapers Ltd', *The Times* (26 March 1954), p.4

33. Subsidiary Company Director's Minutes, 25 June 1952 (LRO: DDVC Acc 7340 Box 27/2)

34. '"Pirouette" in the News', *The Ambassador* (1955), no.1, p.96

35. 'New Deal for Young Teenage Fashion', *Vogue* (April 1955), p.200. Janey Ironside took over from Madge Garland as head of the fashion school at the Royal College of Art in 1956.

36. Horrockses Fashions Limited. Extract from Verbatim Report of the Management Meeting, 25 October 1950 (LRO: DDVC Acc 7340 Box 12/3)

37. Letter from Horrockses to Bert Alston London (CMT firm) (LRO: DDVC Acc 7340 Box 3/4)

38. Horrockses Fashions Limited. Extract from Verbatim Report of the Management Meeting, 27 April 1949 (LRO: DDVC Acc 7340 Box 12/3)

39. Horrockses Fashions Limited. Extract from Verbatim Report of the Management Meeting, 31 January 1952 (LRO: DDVC Acc 7340 Box 12/3)

40. Horrockses Fashions Limited. Extract from Verbatim Report of the Management Meeting, 26 April 1950 (LRO: DDVC Acc 7340 Box 12/3)

41. Iris Ashley, 'I'm Marooned and It's Lovely', *Daily Mail* (13 March 1953) (LRO: DDHs 49/2 1952–55 Newscuttings Book)

42. Investigation into failure of Horrockses Fashions to carry out delivery promises, 1951 (LRO: DDVC Acc 7340 Box 12/3)

43. Letter from Herbert Mallott to Kathleen Molyneux, 2 May 1951 (LRO: DDVC Acc 7340 Box 3/4)

Chapter Four
'Our Best Dresses': The Retail and
Purchase of Ready-to-Wear

1. 'Sloping Shoulders', *Vogue* (March 1941), pp.58–9
2. Angela Partington, 'Popular Fashion and Working Class Affluence', *Chic Thrills: A Fashion Reader* (London, 1992), pp.145–61
3. Wray (1957), p.51
4. Jefferys (1950), p.322
5. Jefferys (1954), p.349
6. Ibid.
7. Ibid. p.93
8. Wray (1957), p.60
9. 'Morrisons Associated Companies Limited', *The Times* (6 May 1948), p.9
10. Jefferys (1954), p.340
11. Worth (2007), p.70
12. Jefferys (1954), p.348
13. Robert Jameson, 'Report on the Fashion Workroom', *Harrodian Gazette* (June 1953), p.231
14. Buruma (2009), p.31
15. Wray (1957), p.180
16. Newby (1970), pp.100–8
17. *Fashions and Fabrics' Brand Survey* (August 1953), p.39
18. Horrockses Fashions Limited. Extract from Verbatim Report of the Management Meeting, 29 June 1949 (LRO: DDVC Acc 7340 Box 12/3)
19. Horrockses Fashions Limited. Extract from Verbatim Report of the Management Meeting, 29 November 1950 (LRO: DDVC Acc 7340 Box 12/3)
20. Horrockses Fashions Limited. Extract from Verbatim Report of the Management Meeting, 29 June 1949 (LRO: DDVC Acc 7340 Box 12/3)
21. Horrockses Fashions Limited. Extract from Verbatim Report of the Management Meeting, 25 January 1950 (LRO: DDVC Acc 7340 Box 12/3)
22. Horrockses Fashions Limited. Extract from Verbatim Report of the Management Meeting, 3 October 1949 (LRO: DDVC Acc 7340 Box 12/3)
23. Register of Retail Outlet Orders 1956–8 (LRO: DDHs 129)
24. Ibid.
25. Accounts Refused, 10 October 1949 (LRO: DDVC Acc 7340 Box 12/3)
26. *Fashions and Fabrics' Brand Survey* (August 1951), p.46
27. Letter from Herbert Mallott to Helena Ashcroft (Town & Country Clothes), 12 December 1951 (LRO: DDVC Acc 7340 Box 3/4)

28. Interview with Ruth Addison, August 1999
29. *Sunday Telegraph* (Australia) (12 June 1955) (LRO: DDHs 49/2 1952–55 Newscuttings Book)
30. Investigation into failure of Horrockses Fashions to carry out delivery promises, 1951 (LRO: DDVC Acc 7340 Box 12/3)
31. Register of Retail Outlet Orders 1956–8 (LRO: DDHs 129)
32. Interview with Daphne Razzell (née Patten), November 2008
33. Isabel Dunjohn, 'Springtime with Horrockses: Dress Show at Bath', *Western Daily Press & Bristol Mirror* (27 January 1954) (LRO: DDHs 49/2 1952–55 Newscuttings Book)
34. Investigation into failure of Horrockses Fashions to carry out delivery promises, 1951 (LRO: DDVC Acc 7340 Box 12/3)
35. 'English Cottons in Dress Corner', *New York Times* (14 June 1955) (LRO: DDHs 49/2 1952–55 Newscuttings Book)
36. Interview with Pat Albeck, November 2000
37. A machinist working in one of Horrockses Fashions' making-up factories earned between £4 and £5 per week.
38. Interview with Jean Moffatt, May 2009
39. Interview with Ruth Addison, August 2009
40. Interview with Joyce Beaumont, August 1999
41. Telephone interview with Ann Parr, April 2009
42. Letter from Irenie Ashwin-Nayler to Horrockses, Crewdson & Co.'s export director, 13 August 1953 (LRO: DDVC Acc 7340 Box 9/3). Ashwin-Nayler comments in the letter that she has been a fashion buyer for 12 years.
43. Interview with Lesley Blackledge, August 1999
44. Interview with Veronica McEvoy, August 1999
45. Interview with Elizabeth Arrowsmith, March 2009
46. Interview with Ruth Addison, August 1999
47. Interview with Peggy Rimmer, May 2009
48. It is doubtful that this was fabric was designed exclusively for Horrockses Fashions and is more likely to be a Horrockses, Crewdson & Co. fashion fabric.
49. Alison Settle, 'A Woman's Viewpoint', *The Observer* (9 November 1952) (LRO: DDHs 49/2 1952–55 Newscuttings Book)
50. 'The Rise of the Ready-to-Wear', *Vogue* (February 1951), p.65

51. Director's report for the year ending 31 August 1946 (LRO: DDVC Acc 7340 Box 22/2)
52. Entwistle (2000), p.3

Select Bibliography

Buruma, Anna, *Liberty and Co. in the Fifties and Sixties: a Taste for Design* (London, 2009)

Carter, Ernestine, *With Tongue in Chic* (London, 1974)

Dawnay, Jean, *Model Girl* (London, 1956)

De la Haye, Amy (ed.), *The Cutting Edge: 50 Years of British Fashion 1947–1997* (London, 1996)

Council of Industrial Design, *Design 46*, (London 1946)

Disher, Margaret, *American Factory Production of Women's Clothing* (London, 1947)

Entwistle, Joanne, *The Fashioned Body: Fashion, Dress and Modern Social Theory* (London, 2000)

Ewing, Elizabeth, *History of 20th Century Fashion* (London, 1974)

Farr, Michael, *Design in British Industry: a Mid-Century Survey* (Cambridge, 1955)

Fashions and Fabrics: Branded Merchandise and Trade Marks Directory, an annual publication produced by *Fashions and Fabrics, Drapery and Fashion Weekly* and published by the National Trade Press

Garland, Ailsa, *Lion's Share* (London, 1970)

Garland, Madge, *Fashion* (London, 1962)

Harden, Rosemary and Turney, Jo, *Floral Frocks: the Floral Printed Dress from 1900 to Today* (Suffolk, 2007)

Haslam, G.A., *Illustrated Book of Draftings: Spring and Summer Coronation Number 23* (London, 1953)

Ironside, Janey, *Janey* (London, 1973)

Jefferys, James, *The Distribution of Consumer Goods: a Factual Study of Methods and Costs in the United Kingdom in 1938* (Cambridge, 1950)

Jefferys, James, *Retail Trading in Britain 1850–1950* (Cambridge, 1954)

Mendes, Valerie and Hinchcliffe, Frances, *Ascher: Fabric, Art, Fashion* (London 1987)

Newby, Eric, *Something Wholesale* (London, 1970)

Palmer, Alexandra, *Couture and Commerce: the Transatlantic Fashion Trade in the 1950s* (Toronto, 2001)

Parrott, William, *The Pictorial Story of HRH The Duchess of Kent's Far East Tour with HRH The Duke of Kent: an Eye Witness Account* (London, 1953)

Pedrick, Gale, *The Story of Horrockses, founded 1791* (Nottingham, 1950)

Pevsner, Nikolaus, *An Enquiry into Industrial Art in England* (Cambridge, 1937)

Rayner, Geoffrey, Chamberlain, Richard and Stapleton, Annamarie, *Artists' Textiles in Britain 1945–1970* (London, 2003)

Reynolds, Helen, 'Pressure and Persuasion: The Board of Trade's Utility Clothing Scheme 1942 to 1945', MA History of Textiles and Dress (Winchester School of Art, 1995)

Rose, Mary B. (ed.), *The Lancashire Cotton Industry: a History Since 1700* (Preston, 1996)

Schoeser, Mary and Boydell, Christine (eds), *Disentangling Textiles: Techniques for the Study of Designed Objects* (London, 2002)

Scott-James, Anne, *In the Mink* (London, 1952)

Sladen, Christopher, *The Conscription of Fashion: Utility Cloth, Clothing and Footwear 1941–52* (London, 1995)

Sparke, Penny (ed.), *Did Britain Make It? British Design in Context 1946–86* (London, 1986)

Wilcox, Claire, *The Golden Age of Couture: Paris and London 1947–57* (London, 2007)

Worth, Rachel, *Fashion for the People: a History of Clothing at Marks & Spencer* (London, 2007)

Wray, Margaret, *The Women's Outerwear Industry* (London, 1957)

Magazines and Journals

The Ambassador
Art and Industry
Country Life
Design
The Drapers' Record
Fashions and Fabrics
Fashions and Fabrics Overseas
Film Fashionland
Harper's Bazaar
The Lady
The Maker-Up
The Queen
Vanity Fair
Vogue
Vogue Book of British Exports
Women's Filmfair
Woman's Journal

Archives and Museum Collections

Archive of Art & Design at the V&A: George Ainscow (AAD/1993/12/1/1); Pat Albeck (AAD/2004/9/68); Joyce Badrocke (AAD/2009/4); John French (AAD/9/1979); Eric Lucking (AAD/8/1986); Betty Newmarch (AAD/1995/16); Frederick Starke (AAD/2000/10)

Abbot Hall Museum & Art Gallery, Kendal: houses Alastair Morton's fabric designs, samples and drawings for Horrockses Fashions
The Bowes Museum, Barnard Castle, County Durham: holds an advertising poster for Horrockses' products
Harris Museum & Art Gallery, Preston (PRSMG): holds the largest collection of Horrockses Fashions' products in Britain
Lancashire Records Office (LRO), Preston: houses a large collection of Horrockses, Crewdson & Co.'s business records, including subsidiaries (DDHs *Records of Horrockses, Crewdson & Co. Ltd*; DDVC Acc 7340 *Additional deposit of records of Horrockses, Crewdson & Co. Ltd*)
Gallery of Costume, Manchester: houses a number of Horrockses Fashions' garments along with a cross-section of other ready-to-wear brands of the 1940s and '50s
Land of Lost Content (http://www.lolc.co.uk/): an online image database
Manchester Metropolitan University, Special Collections: holds the Cotton Board photographic archive
Target Gallery: houses a small collection of Horrockses Fashions' outfits
The Victoria and Albert Museum: holds a small collection of Horrockses Fashions' garments and fabrics designed for the company, as well as examples of couture and ready-to-wear from the period
The Visual Arts Database (VADS) (http://www.vads.ac.uk/): an online resource for the visual arts

Monetary Note

The purchasing power of the pound based on the Bank of England's
Retail Price Index from www.measuringworth.com

1946	£29.73
1947	£29.73
1948	£26.16
1949	£25.45
1950	£24.69
1951	£22.63
1952	£20.72
1953	£20.10
1954	£19.74
1955	£18.88
1956	£18.00
1957	£17.35
1958	£16.84
1959	£16.75
1960	£16.59
1961	£16.04
1962	£15.38
1963	£15.08
1964	£14.60

Pre-decimal (1971)	Post-decimal
1 shilling (s) / 12 old pence (d)	5p
£1 / 240 old pence	£1.00p
1 guinea / £1.1s.	£1.05p

Acknowledgements

I would like to thank the many former employees of Horrockses Fashions who so patiently answered my numerous questions, especially Stephanie Houlgrave and Pat Albeck, who were so helpful at the beginning of this research. I am also grateful to: Pauline Altham, Joyce Badrocke, Sir Terence Conran, Jonny Emakpor, Jean Grinsted, Pamela Lee, Bernard Leser, Gloria Mortimer-Dunn, Daphne Razzell, Marny Shorrocks, and also to Joe David.

The book could not have been written without the memories of the women who wore Horrockses Fashions' outfits, unfortunately a few of them no longer with us: Ruth Addison, Juliet Amery, Elizabeth Arrowsmith, Joyce Beaumont, Lesley Blackledge, Avis Boardman, Beth Hartley, Greta Hetherington, Gillian Jones, Christine Lloyd, Mrs Male, Veronica McEvoy, Virginia McKenna, Jean Moffatt, Constance Morris, Ann Parr, Peggy Rimmer, Wendy Simpson.

Many thanks also to fellow researchers, museum curators and archivists and others who helped along the way: Beatrice Behlen, Richard Chamberlain, Steve Chibnall, Lyn Felscher, Lesley Jackson, Alexia Kirk, Miles Lambert, Maria Lowit, Alexandra MacCullogh, Lesley Miller, Jeremy Parrett, Geoff Rayner, Nick Rogers, Sonnet Stanfill, Philip Sykas, Philip Warren, Eva White, and to staff at the Lancashire Record Office.

Thanks also to Caroline Jordan and the Harris Museum & Art Gallery, Preston; and to Tina Barnes-Powell and colleagues at De Montfort University, Leicester.

To Linda Schofield for fastidious editing, Will Webb for the design. At V&A Publishing, Mark Eastment, Frances Ambler, Clare Davis, and Geoff Barlow.

And finally to Andrew Clay, who now knows more about women's ready-to-wear fashion than he ever thought possible.

Index

Page numbers in *italics* refer to illustrations